Who Did It Now?

My Life with Sled Dogs

Sarah Dobbrastine

First published by Dog Ear Publishing
4010 W. 86th Street, Ste H
Indianapolis, IN 46268
www.dogearpublishing.net

ISBN: 978-1-4575-3270-2

Library of Congress Control Number: has been applied for

This book is printed on acid-free paper.

Printed in the United States of America

Acknowledgments

My family, you have given me your undoubting support since I began this crazy idea of dogsledding. Robyn and Dale, my parents, I can't thank you enough for everything. Words cannot express my gratitude. Adam, thank you for being that shoulder I leaned on when I needed you and thanks for Panda. Lisa, you have been so helpful and that spirit about you is contagious!

To Christina Martin, who gave me the brilliant idea and encouragement to put my stories into writing. Thanks for always being that ear for me to unload on. Love you, girl.

I also want to thank my dogs. They have put up with me through the worst times and through the best. I love you all so much. I can't imagine my life without you guys.

I dedicate this book to my first dog, Toby. You were a light in my life for all the years I had you. You left too soon, but you have inspired me to do what I love for the rest of my life.

CONTENTS

Second Chance Mushers

Sled Dog Rescue

Second Chance Mushers

The Siberian husky and Alaskan malamute can be difficult breeds to own. Second Chance Mushers is a business that I started in the hopes to raise awareness about these breeds, to provide a lifetime experience riding in a dogsled, and to help rescue the ones that are waiting for that forever home. Second Chance Mushers is designed to provide education to the community about these breeds. I want people to understand the requirements that come with these breeds. The more people can understand them, there will be less of a need for me to rescue unwanted dogs.

I know my passion in life is for these dogs. I love being around them, exercising with them, and enjoying life with them. They have a love that is unconditional, they live life in the moment, and they teach us, as humans, how to live life to the fullest.

Riding in a dogsled is one is one of life's best experiences: to feel the excitement of the dogs; the crisp, cold air; and the rush of wind blowing by you as the dogs take off. I want to share that same excitement. It's only an experience you can get behind a team of dogs. You can watch the way they work, the way they take commands, and most of all, how much they love running. My dogs love what they do.

The goal of Second Chance Mushers is to help raise money to provide care, equipment, and food to my current dogs, but to also allow me to help all the others that are in need of homes, as well. I have been offered so many dogs in the past that unfortunately I have had to turn away because financially I could not afford to take on any more dogs. I am hoping with Second Chance Mushers that I can raise money to have available to help pay for the care of the new dogs. I will train them with my team, work on any behavioral problems I see as necessary, then hopefully find them loving forever homes so I may then help the next dogs that come my way.

My goal in writing this story is to allow people who may have been interested in this breed to fully understand their capabilities and their liabilities. I was someone who never researched this breed, I admit. I was intrigued by their beauty, but I soon learned their difficult nature. My hope is to bring awareness to this breed in hopes that people will decide whether this is the right fit for them. I can certainly say that my life would be a lot easier had I selected a different breed, but I know I would not have had as much fun.

I know from my own experience that my dogs tend to wreak havoc when they are not exercised. They want to run, and they will do whatever they need to do to accomplish that goal. Allowing these dogs to release pent-up energy from being inactive will give you a whole new dog. There is nothing better than a relaxed husky that is exhausted from a run.

They are not lapdogs, and they do require grooming. Be prepared. They have a double coat that sheds twice a year. So any dark colors that you like to wear are also going to wear a lot of your dog's hair.

I have seen too many dogs that are not understood and they have to be taken to the shelter. It's really amazing what a different dog you can have with exercise, training, and love. I challenge everyone to go to their local shelter and adopt their next dog. You just might be amazed at what a wonderful, appreciative dog you will get. Life is about second chances: have you gotten yours?

Traveling Down a Different Path

For anyone who loves adventure, exploring, wilderness, and a rush of speed, just one ride on a dogsled is unforgettable. To feel the excitement of the dogs as they are harnessed up, the anticipation of the team building, or the thrill of taking off is something unimaginable. Do I like working all the time and being busy every day of the week? Well, of course not. Is the trade-off worth it? ABSOLUTELY!

Dogsledding is as close to heaven on earth for me. I love that both the dogs and I are doing what we love. Running is the best form of exercise for any Siberian husky or Alaskan malamute. Letting them run full-tilt to their heart's content is so gratifying to watch. I can still recall heading out in the early winter hours when the sun was peering through the trees. It was eerily quiet, you could hear nothing but the soft crunch of the snow beneath each dog's foot, the sled glided softly over the untouched powder, the air was crisp and cold, and it was just the dogs and me.

In the summer hours, the best time is in the morning to take the dogs out. The cart is not as silent as the sled, but the dogs are still as excited as in the winter. We run through the trees while the dew is still covering the forest ground, appearing white in color like snow. We round the corners in the woods, tearing up the ground with each turn we make. We reach a lake at the halfway point, and the dogs are let loose to go for a swim. The team swims around, chasing each other, having the time of their lives. The lake is flat, calm, with no boats or people to bother us. The birds are chirping, the crickets are sounding, and my dogs are splashing all about, destroying the beautiful morning calm. It is a moment in my day that brings such happiness, contentment, and peace. I can think of no other way to begin my day.

Warnings

Siberians and Alaskan malamutes may have stubborn tendencies that can prove to be challenging. They require different regimens to keep them balanced (Siberians more than malamutes). Exercise and discipline are an absolute must in their world. Draining their energy is essential to a happy dog and a happy owner. If you do not follow those two rules, they will dominate your house.

Huskies love to escape at a moment's notice. If a Siberian is left with energy building up day after day, they will become destructive. Destructive...I like to think that's a nice way to put it. (I know many Siberian owners are silently laughing to themselves with that statement.) They eat and steal items from your home, and if you turn your back on them for one second, something is going to be eaten or destroyed. Antics like eating the siding off your house, digging up your newly planted landscaping, or eating a pink highlighter in various areas of your new house are just a few disasters my dogs have caused. They enjoy garbage, pens, furniture, or even a bowl of chili.

A typical attitude of these dogs is, *If I see it, it's mine, if I want it, it's mine, or if it's yours, I want it.* Siberian huskies have this way of looking at you; you can tell that they are truly trying to contemplate what you are thinking. Sometimes they may look at you with complete adoration, but don't be surprised if they have food as an ulterior motive. They are sizing you up, planning their next move when you are least expecting it.

Why Do I Do It?

I am always asked, why you do it? It is time-consuming and costly to own one dog in today's society let alone eight, working two to three jobs at a time while going to school to help pay for the expenses that come with owning them. Why work your life away? My answer is always…because I love it.

Living a life with eight sled dogs can be challenging. One of my beautiful dogs made it impossible to have any windows open, and on those hot, humid, Michigan summer days it became unbearable. She had made it her life goal to see how many windows she could jump out of on any level of my house. I swear she was training for the circus in the off season of dogsledding.

I worked three jobs all summer the year that I bought my first house. It wasn't fun by any means, but I knew what the payoff would be: I would have central air-conditioning. I had to work and save to purchase the equipment necessary and to pay for installation. After six weeks of hell, it finally was Antarctica in northern Michigan; we had central air. The dogs appreciated the air-conditioning so much they'd run quickly outside to go to the bathroom and then they were back in the door before they had a chance to feel the sun on their backs.

Life throws you curveballs and you learn to adjust. Things happen with the dogs that can throw my life off balance, but it doesn't take long for me to bounce back on my feet. That is what makes it life. If it was all laid out in black and white, where would be the fun in that? I am a huge believer that everything happens for a reason, and I know that I am where I am supposed to be, owning all of these dogs.

Anyone who has ever owned a dog before can truly appreciate the never-ending love that they give to you their whole lives. They are there for you when you are at your highest, and they stay right by your side when you are at your lowest. Dogs don't care what you look like, what you wear, or what neighborhood you live in. They do care that you provide them with the love and care they deserve. Dogs love unconditionally until the day they leave this world. They are forgiving and understanding in every way.

My favorite quote, which I like to live by, comes from J.W. Stephens: "Be the person your dog thinks you are." The life lessons these dogs have taught me have carried with me throughout my life. They have shown me how to be independent, resourceful, and most of all, carefree. You could say that owning a dogsled team and rescuing each of the dogs has given me a different outlook on life. I used to be uptight, I took life too seriously, and I never had much fun. Since I have owned these dogs, my life has taken on a different meaning: live each moment like it's your last. Dogs aren't dreading the work meeting in the morning or working long stretches at a time; they just live in the moment, something I now strive to do every day. Life would feel empty without the love of a dog to share it with.

Mushers typically have outside kenneling; a few may come into the house at a time but not usually an entire team. But my dogsled team lives in my house and sleeps on my bed; their kennels are in my basement. Some may say that I am asking for trouble with this lifestyle. I understand that my method may be frowned upon by many, but the dogs and I are happy and that's what matter most.

My First Dogs

What is a day like living with eight sled dogs? Well, to begin the story of how I ended up owning a dogsled team, you need to understand how I have come to own these amazing animals. I grew up a country girl among horses, cows, cats, goats, chickens, and dogs. A love for animals was something that came very naturally to me, and my love has grown into a team of rescued Siberian huskies and Alaskan malamutes. I strongly believe that without the love of my parents and the freedom they gave me to own all these animals, my life would have turned out very differently.

My father's nickname for me was the Pied Piper. Growing up I'd spend most of my time outdoors with the animals. I'd love to play with the cats in the hayloft of our barn, ride horses through the pasture, and play with the collies in the front yard. It wasn't uncommon to see me coming from the barn with a trail of cats following me. But I would have never imagined that growing up surrounded by all these different animals would lead my life to dogsledding.

The first dogs I remember having were our collies, Shogun and Morey. Collies have wonderful temperaments and are terrific as family pets. Collies are very different-natured from Siberians or malamutes. They are patient, gentle, and listen very well.

Shogun

Shogun was a large boy who carried the gentlest of hearts. He loved being around people and the attention that they would give him. He was a large boy with a beautiful flowing coat of deep black, tan, and white. His gentle nature made him safe around other animals and people of all ages. A child could step on him, pull his hair, or take a bone from his mouth and he would not bat an eyelash. He lived his life roaming through my parents' property in the country, never straying far from home. He would enjoy an occasional romp through the woods, but he never was gone long or went far.

He had long hair that allowed many things to become intertwined in it—leaves, twigs, and mud—that would dry and matt before he came home. This would make it extra fun when he would decide to venture into the woods and become one with his surroundings. I am sure many of you who own dogs can relate to the gut-wrenching feeling of knowing you are going to spend the next day combing them out. He would come back massively tangled in burrs, and it would have been easier to just shave him, but instead we would spend hours combing him out.

We had so many dog brushes that it was more like a surgical operation after a while and I had all the brushes down at a very young age. "Curry comb?"—"STAT"; "Undercoat rake?"—"STAT"; "And scissors?"—"STAT." There was a brush that worked on large burrs, a brush that worked well on "this kind" of burr, and there was an excellent finishing brush to remove the smaller burrs. Becoming an expert burr remover by the age of ten became my forte.

Like many things as we age, our body begins to function in ways that only it decides; this applies to dogs, as well. As he grew older, the scent of Shogun's breath was only comparable to that of something that had been decaying in the hot sun for over a week. Shogun loved to give kisses, and he never cued in on the unwillingness of his human owners to receive those gifts. My brother would have both my arms pinned down to the side, with my two legs kicking with all their might, and then proceed to call Shogun over. This left no escape from Shogun and his breath. I was usually on the losing end of this trick and could only seem to get my brother when it was by complete surprise or I had the assistance of an older adult.

But even with his breath, Shogun created a love, passion, and understanding of canines that little did I know would play a large role in my life decisions. He turned that light bulb on in my head that allowed me to see the devotion and bond a dog can have with a human. My active lifestyle is more compatible to that of a dog than that of the cats I had spent so much time with as a child.

Shogun died at an old age of unknown causes. He wandered off one day and remained gone a lot longer than he usually did. Days went by before we eventually did find him. He was brought back home and laid to rest at my parents' house in the country in a private spot in our deep backyard. Shogun was a wonderful, handsome, and caring dog. He set the standard high for the dogs that followed in his paw prints.

Shogun's Life Perspective

I grew up on a quiet farm out in the country. I had acres of wooded land and ponds in which to spend my days leisurely exploring. There weren't any schedules or deadlines to live by—life was just free. I frolicked around, rolled in the green grass, and then explored the woods from time to time. There I was free to go about my life as I chose. I never roamed far or for long because my people seemed to worry when I did that, so I just kept close to home.

I grew up with the most loving of families. I had two big people who provided food and water for me. Then there were three little children who loved to have me chase them and give them kisses. The people didn't seem too happy with me when I came back from my excursions in the woods. They seemed to complain a lot when I came back at how awful I looked. I did feel a little tightness of my coat and knew things were stuck in it, but I didn't mind. It added character, I would say. The next thing I knew, I had two people with sticks in their hands running them up and down my coat. They did this for hours. Sometimes I'd think, *Are we done? I need to use the bathroom.* I was a patient dog so I waited kindly until they were exhausted of this activity and left me alone.

The two larger of the children loved to play outside. They could play for hours in the lawn and in the woods. I've seen the battle-of-all-battles water fights where they even had shields to protect themselves from the water. I didn't see what the big deal was; water was great! "Get soaked, kids!" They usually carried these long hoses and sprayed

water out of the end at each other. Loud screaming was usually followed by the water, especially from the young girl. I didn't mind the
bloodcurdling scream because it was so much fun to run around with
them.

That boy and girl sure did love to play games with each other.
There was one game that they always included me in, and I loved it.
They would chase each other around the front yard screaming and
giggling. Usually the girl was on the losing end of this game, and
when the boy would catch her, he would sit on her and hold her arms
down. That's where I would come in. The boy would call me over to
give that little girl all the kisses I could possibly manage to give. Sometimes the girl would have help from an adult, and they could hold
down the boy and then I would perform my magic. I sure did love
those summer days playing with them in the yard. That's what life is
about for a dog: family, home, and a soft bed.

Morey

The collies that I grew up with were the best family dogs we could have ever owned. Morey was our female that we raised alongside Shogun. She was a beautiful blond-and-white, gentle-natured girl. She had deep brown eyes that were always consoling when I needed to wrap my arms around her and lay my head against hers to cry on. Morey was a birthday present for my older brother, Adam, from my grandmother Emery. Morey's name came from the T-shirt my brother was wearing on his birthday that said, "Morey Boogie." He was young at the time and so the name Morey stuck.

Morey had two things in life that would always ignite a flame inside her and get her riled up. The first was a single phrase. My brother one day said to her, "I drive a Volvo," and she went nuts. Who knew that something so simple and silly would be her favorite? I am sure many of you are now thinking, *Yes, I have a saying that I use with my dog.* It would become a game we would play using this saying. When we said it, she would come sprinting from wherever she was. How my brother came to saying that to her is still unknown to me. Dogs do react to the tone of voice and body language, which could have been influencing her, as well, but we will never know. Dogs want nothing more than to please their owners, so good ol' Morey went along with them.

The other thing that Morey would obsess about was the lawn mower. It didn't seem to matter what type of lawn mower it was, just the start-up of the engine put her into a barking frenzy. She would come running from anywhere she was just to bark uncontrollably at the large heap of metal. Then, as soon as it set in motion, the fun was over and she would carry on with whatever she had been doing before. We were young and didn't know much about dog behavior, but we would entertain ourselves for hours by starting up the lawn mower and watching our Morey in action. Then we'd shut it down and do it all over again. Cheap country entertainment for two young kids, I guess. Even in her old age, Morey continued on with her behaviors, making our lives as young kids a lot of fun.

Morey became the first inside dog I ever owned. She spent most of her life as an outside dog. This is where I became intrigued and fell in love with the idea of spending most of my time with a dog around. I loved this way of life so much that it changed the way I lived with dogs from that point on.

Morey lived a long and happy life with my family. She grew old and died a happy girl, but not before she taught a few life lessons to the Siberian huskies that she lived with.

A View from Morey's World

Well, I would not say that my introduction was very ladylike. I was kept in a crate, hidden in some little girl's room. I sat there and waited for what seemed like days but probably was only hours, and then some lady finally came and got me. She put a large bow around my neck and I was finally free. I was taken to a large living room where there were a lot of people. In the middle of the room sat a little boy. He had his eyes closed and was being told to keep them closed by the big people. The lady placed me at his feet. The entire room counted to three, and then he opened his eyes. He let out a loud gasp, and then he grabbed me so tight I could barely breathe. So this is what being loved was like!

I realized quickly that this was my new home. This little boy was going to take care of me. I was passed around that day to every human in the room. I got so much loving I didn't know what to do. Most of the people soon all left, and only two big people and three kids remained. The little boy kept saying the same word over and over to me: Morey. I decided I would go to him and see what he wanted so badly. It was then I realized that my name was Morey! How amazing was that? I had a name!

Well, I needed to relieve myself and so the little boy took me out to an area of large green grass. I ran and ran until I couldn't run anymore. This new place was huge! Then out of nowhere a large boy dog came over. He looked like me but had darker hair. He was so nice to me, and he told me he would show me the ropes of the new place. His name was Shogun. Shogun took me to all of his hiding places and the stomping grounds around this new house I lived in. He taught me how to splash through the ponds, chase deer in the woods, and get these sticky things stuck in your fur! The people did not care for those at all, and I had to sit forever while they removed those sticky things. It was all worth it, though.

The people drove a loud machine around all over the grass. The sound of it starting up drove me crazy. I would try to warn them about starting it by running over to it and barking as loud as I could, but it didn't stop them. It would start to run loudly, and then they drove it back and forth across the lawn. They would do this one to two times a week, and it was very disturbing. I put forth a valiant effort to stop it every time, but I always failed. I still loved my human people though, despite them driving this irritating loud machine.

That young boy one day started to say things that I had never heard before. He would say, "I drive a Volvo!" I just loved it. It could have been foreign or slang, but it didn't matter because I loved the sound of it. I have no idea why, but I loved it and could listen to him say those words all day long. He would say it in such a high-pitched tone and have such a huge grin on his face that I couldn't help but come running. Even when I had reached old age and could barely hear the sound of anything else, I could hear that. I loved that boy so much.

Life was great living out in the country. I had Shogun to spend my time with when the people needed to go away, and then I got lots of love when they came home. My life was great, and I couldn't imagine spending it any other way.

The First Husky

Collies have very different personality traits than those of the Siberian husky and Alaskan malamute. So my family was somewhat blindsided by the antics that these northern breeds could perform when they became a part of my life. It wasn't until I was in high school that my devotion became focused on these northern breeds.

Cody

After Shogun passed away, we decided Morey needed a companion. She wasn't acting lonely, but I think as a family we liked having two dogs around. This was when my family began our adventure with the Siberian husky breed.

I had just started high school, and we were going on a trip to find our new family member. My father, brother, sister, and I traveled three hours downstate to a kennel that bred Siberian huskies. We were fascinated with the appearance of the Siberian husky, but we did not research the breed like we should have. I am sure many Siberian owners understand that instant first love of their piercing blue eyes, the dark masks on their faces, and their ability to look right through you. It's not until the puppy becomes an adolescent that you realize the trouble you are in. The amount of energy, time, and money we invest in our pets can be astounding.

Cody was the first young male Siberian that we purchased from a breeder. He was a young black, silver, and white, medium-built male with bright blue eyes. We raised him inside the house, while the elderly Morey meandered a little lethargically around at her own pace. Cody adapted to her behavior for a while by keeping close to the house and not wandering off. It wasn't until he began to mature into an adult that his husky independence began to emerge—in the form of running away from home.

The Siberian husky trait of roaming and wandering began to emerge in Cody when he -was around one year of age. Our house was settled in the midst of twenty-six acres of trees and about one half mile from the road, but this didn't slow him down any. One early summer morning, Cody experienced horrendous injuries when he crossed paths with an oncoming vehicle. He suffered serious injuries, but he survived.

His biggest injury was a broken right hip. A metal rod was inserted to stabilize the joint while it healed. Our vet warned us to keep an eye on the hip and to keep his movement limited. Trying to keep a young male Siberian at limited movement is not the easiest task. Cody would try to run around the yard at any chance he got, so we were forced to leash him up each time we went out. The leash would be jerked in all different directions as he made every attempt to break free. He eventually returned to the vet to have the rod removed after enough time had passed for the bone to heal. After countless checkup appointments with the vet, pain medications, surgeries, antibiotics, blood transfusions, and constant supervision, Cody eventually made a full recovery and returned to his normal life.

Cody never learned from his ordeal, and sadly he met his fate on that same country road on a weekday morning in early spring. The fog had settled, there was dew on the ground, and I had just awakened to go to school. I still remember going out to the kitchen and seeing the looks on my parents' faces. My heart sank to my stomach. I knew it was Cody. They told me that he was gone and there was no life-saving surgery that could have saved him, not this time. I collapsed to the ground, laid my head in my lap, and just let the tears flow. My parents hugged me and held me tightly, and they, too, were crying alongside me. It took weeks to get over the loss of Cody. Eventually, I could talk about him without crying but it took time.

The Rainbow Bridge

"The Rainbow Bridge" is a poem written by an anonymous author that talks about where our pets go when they pass away. It provides comfort and assurance that they are safe and happy while waiting for their owners to return to them.

Just this side of heaven is a place called Rainbow Bridge. When an animal dies that has been especially close to someone here, that pet goes to Rainbow Bridge. There are meadows and hills for all of our special friends so they can run and play together. There is plenty of food, water, and sunshine, and our friends are warm and comfortable. All the animals who had been ill and old are restored to health and vigor; those who were hurt or maimed are made whole and strong again, just as we remember them in our dreams of days and times gone by. The animals are happy and content, except for one small thing; they each miss someone very special to them, who had to be left behind. They all run and play together, but the day comes when one suddenly stops and looks into the distance. His bright eyes are intent; his eager body quivers. Suddenly he begins to run from the group, flying over the green grass, his legs carrying him faster and faster.

You have been spotted, and when you and your special friend finally meet, you cling together in joyous reunion, never to be parted again. The happy kisses rain upon your face; your hands again caress the

beloved head, and you look once more into the trusting eyes of your
pet, so long gone from your life but never absent from your heart.
Then you cross Rainbow Bridge together....

Cody joined the many loved pets that have passed and have traveled to "The Rainbow Bridge." My memories of him will never fade; I will always remember him as the dog that stole my heart and began my love for the breed of the Siberian husky. This would change my life forever.

Cody's Life Outlook

The day I arrived at my new home was so wonderful. There were three young kids and two big people who brought me to a place in the country. There were so many smells there that awoke so many senses in my little puppy body. I scrambled as fast as I could out of the little girl's arms so I could explore the new place they had brought me to. I landed on the soft, plush green grass and ran as fast as my legs could take me.

There was the smell of another dog there, too, but I couldn't find her. I was looking and running, but I still couldn't find her. But when I ran quickly back to the people, there she was. She was a blonde, not like me, and older. Her name was Morey, she told me, and she had lived there for a very long time. She explained how we had so much to do and so many places to explore. The food was great, and we would always have fresh water available for us.

I noticed early on that Morey always stuck close to home. She didn't want to run as far and as long as I could or like I wanted to. I followed her lead and remained around the house as long as I could. But one day I thought, *Why not? Let's go exploring a little farther.* I ran as fast as I could down the driveway until I reached more concrete. The concrete went in both directions and I couldn't decide where I wanted to go. I ventured off to the right and ran as fast as my legs could take me. It was an amazing feeling to stretch my legs to their fullest ability. The wind whipped past me, smells were all around me, and I was flying. All of a sudden, out of nowhere I felt an extreme pain and I tumbled off the concrete into the grass. I looked up and a large piece of metal was rumbling right in front of me. A human got out and ran to my side. He looked at my collar and then pulled something out of his pocket. It made a few beeping sounds and then it stopped. The next thing I knew, my people were there and were picking me up and putting me into their own piece of rumbling metal.

We drove down the road. I was hurting, but they were talking to me in such comforting voices, telling me to hang on and that it was going to be okay. I was so comforted to know they were there with me. The rumbling metal machine stopped, and they scooped me up and took me into a building. The smells of animals flooded my senses, and I knew I was somewhere that people helped furry people like me.

I was taken back into a room and placed on a cold metal stand. They gave a small pinch in my front leg, and I felt so much relief from the pain. I don't remember much after that except waking up in a cage and feeling groggy. Slowly I got my bearings and realized I was still at the animal place. I remained there through feeding time, and then they took me out on a leash to a grassy area to go to the bathroom. I was stiff and sore, but they gave me treats that helped with the pain so much. I slept through the night, and then my people came to get me.

When I went home, I was always kept on a leash after that. But I was sore and had no desire to want to run anyway. Morey stayed with me and lay by my side while I slept in and out through the days. She told me I should never go back to that concrete world because it was not safe, and I knew she was right. I never wanted to feel that pain again.

I always would have that urge and desire to want to run and explore, but Morey was a constant reminder for me to stay close to what is familiar. The people provided a wonderful world for me, and I loved them so much. I will keep my running to my dreams, where the rumbling metal machines do not exist.

More Huskies

Rocky

Our family did decide to get another dog, and we soon found a young male Siberian husky and Alaskan malamute mix whom we named Rocky. During my high school years, when the Worldwide Wrestling Federation was a huge hit, the favorite character of my siblings and me was of course "The Rock." It didn't take us long to decide what to name our new dog, and for once we were all in agreement. My family selected the name Rocky, a modified version of "The Rock."

Rocky came from a breeder who raised Alaskan malamutes and Siberian huskies at her home. As we pulled up to the house, I saw that a large privacy fence encircled the front of the property. Once inside the fence, I saw many large kennels that housed many different-looking dogs. Some of the dogs were Alaskan malamutes and some were Siberian huskies. The dogs were of many colors and sizes. There were red dogs, white dogs, black dogs, and silver dogs. Rocky was selected out of a litter of puppies. He himself helped us pick him because he was the only one showing interest in us. The other puppies were just running around, jumping and playing with each other.

When Rocky first arrived, Morey was about eleven years old and less energetic than him, but he still followed her lead. Her calmness helped to keep him around the house and prevented him from running off. Sadly, Morey eventually had a severe stroke and we had to make that heartbreaking decision every pet owner dreads. Humanely euthanizing a dog is the kindest way to end their suffering. It is a difficult decision, but it involves the owner being less selfish and doing what's best for their pet. We determined the most comfortable way to do this was to have the vet come to our house, where she was the most comfortable. Her suffering was then ended; she found peace and took her place beside Shogun. With her passing, Rocky no longer had a mentor around to show him proper dog behavior. From there on out, Rocky became my first challenge by testing the limits of running away any chance he could.

Rocky was the one to introduce us to the Siberian husky independence, which some like to call stubbornness. Rocky's wonderful Siberian behavior did not take place until we added a second addition to our family, a young eight-week-old red female Siberian husky. He was about a year old when the new dog joined our family. Rocky still remained around the house for months to come, until he grew old into his manhood, but then he discovered the urge to wander and fulfill his need for running. He loved sprinting off, like he was slamming a gas pedal down and holding it there for miles! Rocky loved to just let it all out and run!

Rocky mastered the art of evading capture on his first outing. He would take off and purposely not come to us when we came into close distance of him. I call it the Siberian husky taunt, which I am sure all husky owners have experienced at one time or another. The look they give is as if they are laughing at you when they run off.

From Rocky's antics, my father learned the value of recruiting and he asked our neighbor to join him in his search mission, knowing Rocky would not come to us because (1) he knew he was in trouble, and (2) we would take him right back home where he would have to plot his next escape all over again. But Rocky loved to meet new people, so we incorporated that strategy into his capture. Once they had Rocky in sight, our neighbor got out of my dad's truck and called Rocky over to the vehicle, and he gladly came. Our neighbor coaxed him into our truck, where my father was hiding crouched under the seat like a cougar waiting to pounce on his prey. When the door was shut and there was no chance for escape, he came face-to-face with my father. Rocky's pupils were huge, he was panting heavily, but that all stopped the moment he laid eyes on my father. He almost had to do a double take as if he couldn't believe he'd fallen for that. His mouth closed, his ears went flat against his head, and he knew the fun was over. If dogs could talk, I imagine a few choice words would have escaped his mouth at that moment.

I developed my own strategies for capturing that troublemaker. Once he escaped out the door when I wasn't paying attention. Rocky was smart, but I was smarter. I knew I could only capture him with food, so I grabbed a handful of cheese slices on my way out the door. I jumped into my car, flew down the driveway, and followed him in hot pursuit down the road. I managed to pull my car to the right of him and then put some distance between us. I rolled down my window and threw the cheese slices onto the concrete. Now, Rocky's stomach has always been bigger than his brain. When he stopped to gobble them up, I grabbed him.

Rocky became our first test candidate for the system of invisible fencing. We started this journey with a two-prong collar. We put him through the basic training regimen of walking the boundary and letting him identify his boundary flags. It didn't take him long to recognize that when he heard the "beep, beep" and saw the flag, it meant he was too close to the boundary and he should head back toward the house. He obeyed the sound of the collar during his training course when he was on a leash. But this training technique would only prove to work with him when he was on a leash, thus making the entire system a waste of money and time.

Rocky always had a look he gave you when you were -calling him to come back to the house. It was as if he was laughing inside because he knew what he was going to do and we were not going to stop him. Rocky soon came to the realization that if he ran very fast, he would only have to endure the pain of a few jolts and then he would be free. So this began our invisible fence challenge. The fence always then had to be powered down so he could return back over the line if we were not successful in catching him.

We eventually had another consultation with the company that installed the fencing. A special trainer was brought out to make an attempt to retrain Rocky to obey the boundaries of the fence. Needless to say, it took a valiant effort on the trainer's part. Siberians have a very thick coat, especially around the region of the neck. Rocky soon had a charming shaved line around his neck to ensure that he was feeling the invisible fence collar every time he passed through the line. It was our assumption that he was just not feeling the effects of the collar. Soon, when he did make his escape attempts, it was obvious to us by his head twitching to the side over and over as he ran, that he was indeed feeling the collar. Still, the pain of the fence was nothing compared to the freedom that awaited him on the other side.

Rocky took off, time and time again. For a third time the company was brought back out in an attempt to keep Rocky within the perimeter of the fence. A four-prong collar was introduced, and Rocky was again put through his training regimen daily. Every day my family and I would walk Rocky around the perimeter, let him see the flags in the ground, make sure he could hear the sound of the beep as he got close to one, then praised him whenever he backed away. But it never worked for long. Rocky, at this point, was developing a plan of escape each time, but when he took off he was just like a pack of dogs running after a three-legged cat and soon he was gone, leaving his entire family to have go out pacing the country side after him.

We began to look suspicious in our vehicles, creeping slowly around the neighbors' houses, flashers on, each of us on our cell phone asking if the other had seen him, and hollering for our dog. It was like a mob had taken over the Laingsburg countryside. Our neighbors at one point thought we were out planning to rob the neighborhood and they brought their guns outside. "Forget the cops, we have rifles," they said. This is normal behavior for those who live in the middle of nowhere. Soon our neighbors realized that if they ever saw the dark green truck, dark gray SUV, and white car, it was just the Dobbrastines looking for one of their dogs…again.

The company made one last attempt to help Rocky stay within the parameters of the invisible fence, a belly shocker. The thought and sound of this device was very menacing, and our family decided NOT to use it, much to the happiness of my father. The trainer then suggested strapping a weight to a leash on a harness that Rocky would wear. The goal would be to slow him down long enough to feel the invisible fence and deter him from leaving. We soon realized that it actually slowed him down after he crossed the line and it made our attempts to catch him easier. As time passed, though, Rocky grew stronger and we had to keep increasing the weight he would be pulling. We would chuckle to ourselves often, imagining Rocky pulling up the driveway with his weights to the theme song to *Rocky*. It quickly became a rule that Rocky could never be allowed off his leash.

One day while bringing Rocky out from the house, my father had his hands full. In an attempt to keep Rocky in place while he unloaded his arms, he attached him to our garbage tote. It was the short, fat, dark green container with the two wheels attached to the back and a handle on the front that made it the perfect place to tie Rocky up to. While grabbing Rocky's weights, my father then turned his back. He realized then that Rocky was missing along with the garbage tote. Hoping it wouldn't be too difficult to find him, my family and I set out with our cell phones and cars. While heading down the driveway, we noticed far off to the right where the garbage tote had lodged itself between two trees on the other side of the retaining wall. Rocky was stuck. It was the only successful device we ever attached to him that kept him within the parameters of the yard; however, we needed our garbage tote and we could not keep him attached to it as a preventive measure, so back to the harness and weights he went.

Rocky was always our comical one. He had a permanent smile pinned to his goofy face. He also had a thing for one of my best friends, Jovonnah. Something about her was just appealing to him. One night after we had all been swimming in our pool, Jovonnah and her brother were saying good-bye in our driveway and Rocky strolled up to her. He was acting casual and sniffed around her legs and feet. We did not think much of it. But before we realized what was happening, Rocky lifted his leg in the air and peed all over her. I gasped in shock and she jumped back in astonishment. Rocky crouched down to the ground as if to say, "I'm so sorry. I didn't know any better." I knew he did know better, but his reaction made us all laugh despite our being mortified. Thank goodness for understanding friends. Thankfully, that was his only episode of urinating on humans—but it wasn't Rocky's only encounter with Jovonnah.

While vacationing up north, Jovonnah accompanied my family and me. Rocky chose this occasion to develop a desire to find items and shred them. Jovonnah's belongings were the first items to fall victim to his new interest. Jovonnah had a great pair of casino pattern, silky underwear that, if I recall, were among her favorites. Rocky made the decision that they were going to be his favorite pair, as well. We left him unsupervised in the house and soon Jovonnah's casino underwear were ravished into shreds all over my bedroom. He showed no mercy: he shredded, and shredded, and shredded until there was nothing left to shred. I bet many of you are now picturing that moment when you discovered your first pair of shredded underwear. I felt horrible, but I could not stop laughing at the strangeness of the situation. Rocky thereafter had a desire to find underwear from anyone and make them his.

Over the years Rocky developed a special way of letting us know when his stomach was speaking for him. He would come into my parents' living room, sit at my father's feet, and stare him down. He was not doing this to be a mean dog, but next to my father on a stand was a jar of dog cookies. Rocky would avert his attention long enough to make his point known, staring at the cookie jar and then back to my father. His gaze was so eerily still and his mouth was closed, not blinking, just staring. You couldn't help but laugh and give in. Yes, I know that this was not proper training for a dog, but my family has always had too soft of hearts for dogs. This was how Rocky developed the nickname "Chubby."

Rocky stole the hearts and attention of anyone he met. He was getting up to the age of seven when he started to attend a doggie daycare where I worked. He soon became a weekly visitor. He did enjoy the attention and the chance to meet other dogs, but his overall favorite part of daycare was the attention he received from the other staff members, specifically the owner. She soon learned, as well, that the true secret to Rocky's heart was food. She would whisper to him often, "Do you want a cookie?" His ears would perk up, his mouth would close, and his big, round eyes would stare intently at her. She would lead him quietly through a door and sneak him a cookie in the break room. When he was finished, out the door he would trot, so proud that he had been selected to receive a cookie all by himself without interruption from the other dogs. Rocky was a loveable dog, and he won the hearts of everyone he met.

Rocky was an outsider, and he had no one to play with while he was there. Play pools were set up during the summer hours to help the dogs cool down and relax. Rocky was never much of a water dog. He did, however, one day decide to venture into one of the kiddie pools that were set out. As he would enter a pool that had dogs in it, they would all disperse one by one, leaving him all alone. This continued over and over and over. He would pool hop among the three pools in the play yard, and with each pool he entered, the dogs would disperse. It never seemed to discourage him, but it seemed to become a game. It was obvious the other dogs did not like his presence, but they didn't stop him, either. He was slow, not bounding from pool to pool, which made it even more comical. Rocky was never one for liking water, so why this game continued on I do not know.

Rocky lived to the old age of twelve. He ran as a member on my dogsled team until the age of nine, when he then retired to couch life. He lived with me for one year in Traverse City, but when he retired, he returned to the countryside where he was raised. One evening Rocky did not have much of an appetite, which was very unusual for him. It was late at night, and he would only eat a few cookies that were offered. If he was not better in the morning, the plan was to take him to the veterinarian. He slept through the night and was placed into the kennel that morning, going about his business. He was eating cookies, drinking water, and performing his usual daily activities. We thought all had returned to normal and that maybe it was just a stomach bug. But when my father returned from work that afternoon, Rocky was found lying peacefully on the ground. He had slipped away through the day and traveled to the Rainbow Bridge. There he was limitless, with no boundaries. He is now free to live life as he had always wanted. But…he is waiting.

Cookie? (Rocky's Story)

The day I met this wonderful family I knew it would be life changing. They were just as excited to see me as I was to see them. When they brought me to my new home, I was welcomed by an older dog named Morey. She was really nice and very wise. Morey taught me the ropes of the place and the amazing fun things to do. She was reserved and wise, and she taught me a lot about life.

I could sense that there had been something sad that had happened there recently. Morey explained to me how Cody had left unexpectedly. She warned me of the concrete jungle and the pain that a rumbling, metal machine can cause. I was sticking with her. I didn't want to feel the pain they felt or experience the sadness that they all were feeling.

Morey and I would become best buds. She was my leader and my mentor. I learned how to behave in a house, not beg for food, and how to earn cookies. Oh, how I loved cookies. They were the best thing in the entire world. I learned that if I sat, shook hands, lay down, or stayed, I could earn a cookie. When my people came around, I would try to perform all my tricks in hopes of a cookie. I realized that these people weren't always carrying cookies and I didn't see why not. I loved them and they should have always carried bags of them around.

Morey grew very old in the time that I knew her. One day she got so sick that the animal doctor had to come to the house to visit her. The next thing I knew, Morey was gone. I was so sad and so were my people. Morey had been with them for so long. She had told me so many stories of things she had seen and done with them. She loved them and they loved her. What was I going to do without my best friend?

I grew lonely very quickly without Morey. Morey was the glue in my life that kept me close to home when my wandering thoughts would come. When she went to the Rainbow Bridge, I decided I wanted to explore the world. I started out with small ventures and would come back in a few hours. My people would be outside yelling my name. I could hear them, but there were so many sights and sounds to experience that I didn't want to go back yet. Running, running, and running was the best feeling in the world. To feel your legs and lungs burn with exhaustion was the life of a Siberian husky.

My people didn't seem too fond of my new wandering technique. One day they had a man come to our house, and he walked behind a rumbling, metal machine that was smaller than the other rumbling, metal machines but just as loud. Then a lady came out to the house and talked to my people for a while. She then put a collar on my neck super tight. I was like, "I can't breathe, lady, loosen it up a bit." They then put me on a leash and walked me around a path that the rumbling, metal machine had made. It was marked with cute little flags that formed an invisible line. I heard a loud beep and then she would turn me back toward the house, yipping, "Yeah, yeah, yeah, good boy, good boy." I didn't get it at first, but then I realized that the beep meant I needed to go back toward the house. *Okay, lady, I will play your game for a while, but when you are not looking, all bets are off if I don't start getting some cookies.*

One day they were walking me along the new line in the ground where the beeping sound lived, and I thought I would make my best effort to go past the line in the ground because I wanted to explore. It was quick, I was strolling, and then it happened. A sharp, pinching feeling started around my neck and I wanted to run away from it. I darted toward the house, and then they did it again: "Good boy, yeah, yeah, yeah." I was so confused. I get a zap in the neck, run away from it, and I was a good boy? It was when the cookies were introduced into the mix that I decided this wasn't a bad deal. With each beep and turn toward the house, I'd get a cookie. I liked that deal. Beep, turn, cookie. Beep, turn, cookie. I nailed it by the twentieth time, which meant twenty cookies for me.

Once I had finally proved that I knew the line in the ground was home to the beepers, they let me off my leash to roam free. When I'd wander toward the land of the beepers, I'd turn around and go another direction. One day I thought, *Why not? Let's go past the land of the beepers and see what's out there.* I got a little pinch in my neck and then nothing. Yahoo, I was free! I was going to run, run, and run with nobody stopping me.

Before I knew it, I had a herd of rumbling, metal machines hounding after me as I ran through the concrete jungle. They were yelling my name while riding the machines, but I didn't want to listen because I was running. There were times when they would be walking up to me and I wanted to keep playing, so why not with them? I would hold still so I would let them think I wasn't going to move, and then, bam! I'd take off with them running in hot pursuit after me. Ha ha, suckers! That was usually when you could catch me with the biggest grin on my face. I could sense their irritation with me, but gosh, I loved that game of chase. The energy they could emit sometimes made me think they did not like the game chase as much as I did.

When I would finally let them capture me, they would put me into the metal machine and take me home. This time they put a harness on me and strapped heavy objects to it and made me drag it around. It slowed me down a lot and I wasn't fast enough to get through the land of the beepers and the land of the zappers fast enough. So I decided I would meander around the lawn pulling my weights. It was okay, though, because I was bulking up for the ladies.

People owned the softest pieces of cloth ever. They lay on soft cloths, they dressed in soft cloths, and they slept in soft cloths. Some of them were so soft they would drive me absolutely crazy to the point that I just needed to shred them because I didn't know what else to do. People should try it sometime; it was intoxicating. My people would just leave them lying around on the ground sometimes, making it so accessible to me. I couldn't help myself! It was like dangling a steak in front of me and not expecting me to eat it, okay, people?

One of the people always went to this place filled with dogs. It was so much fun. I would get there before all the other dogs, which allowed me to have the upper hand. They were new coming in, and I could smell them first. Hey, I was there first. I had seniority.

That place was amazing. I got to hang out with all these dogs and people who were so excited to see me. Of course, one of my people was always there, but the others there loved me, too. One in particular would sneak me through side doors for cookies. It was awesome, and then she would sneak me back out. Like Batman and Robin we made quite the team.

All that time working out with my weight set at home was finally paying off. I had so many babes checking out my finely, tuned biceps. I would work on my tan in the pool all day and chase the girls from time to time. What can I say? Life is rough when you are a Rocky.

One particular person of mine spent more time with me than the others. She believed in exercise where I believed in cookies. She liked to hook me up next to my family of canines and make me pull her around all the time. I wish she could have understood me because she thought I was lazy, but there she was making me pull her? Lady, you got it all wrong. How about I hook you up to a harness and have you pull me?

Overall, I can't complain. I have a great place to live, amazing loving people, and I get to take many trips to Dogville. It is a great life, and I love every hot-chase, fabric-ripping, cookie-eating moment of it. Did you say cookie?

Teeka

Teeka was a beautiful red female husky that we got shortly after Morey left our lives. It became clear as she began to grow that there was a special connection between Rocky and Teeka that would last through their lives. Teeka was from a German racing sled team, which basically means that the drive to run was bred into her. Her intelligence as one of my lead dogs has never been surpassed by any other dog I have ever owned. Teeka would drop her shoulder into the other lead dog beside her to get it to move in the direction I commanded if they were not listening. She is also the most independent dog that we have ever owned.

Teeka had the escape tactic down at a very young age. To this day we are still not clear how as a puppy she managed to crawl under the garage door, but she did. The garage doors were electric. Even though each was a single car door, they were still quite heavy. It was fall so we were at school and work during the day. My brother was the first to return home, and Teeka was found wedged under the garage door. In the process of attempting to squirm out, she broke her leg. Luckily this injury occurred when she was only about two months old, so she was able to heal quickly. Her leg did heal over time and she never was fazed by it. It was difficult to keep a two-month-old Siberian husky quiet, but we managed. Teeka eventually did calm down over the years and developed into a wonderful, loving dog.

Teeka did have her moments when she would test my patience because the Siberian independent nature would come out. She was smart, elegant, and very independent. She enjoyed her time alone, away from the other dogs. Teeka was the alpha dog among my pack. She was my only female for a very long time. She loved to be outside. She would come inside for the night along with the other dogs, but within a half hour she was restless and crying, requesting to go back outside. If it was the wintertime, you could guarantee that she would not come inside. She loved the winter, and the lower the temperature, the harder it was to get that girl inside. She did what she wanted, when she wanted, and on her terms. Teeka was unique in that way.

Teeka was always a superb lead dog. She had run most of her life and was the only female dog on a team of four. She ran with Rocky and her two pups. The main problem I had with her was making her stay. The drive she had when she was running has never compared to any other dog I have ever owned.

My dogs had never been ones to be let off the leash. They had a strong desire to run and would take off quickly. I would lead the dogs out of my SUV two at a time and hook them to my sleigh. The snow hook is an iron claw that I slam into the snow with my foot to anchor the sled when I need to step off of it. It weighs about twenty pounds and is difficult to become dislodged. I recall a day when I thought I anchored my snow hook into the ground properly, but Teeka soon proved me wrong. She had been paired up with another dog to run lead with her. He was being trained for the lead position alongside her. I had just hooked them up to the sled when I turned my back. The snow hook was pulled out of the snow, and they took off with my sled through the woods. My only luck at that point was knowing I had strapped two sets of jingle bells to the sled, so I could at least be able to hear the direction the sled was heading in.

Panic was setting in at that point. Horrible versions of what could happen ran through my mind. Would they get hurt, or tangled in the line? Was my sled going to be in one piece? It was my first month owning that dogsled, and it was my first sled ever. As a poor college student, it had taken months to save up to buy it. I would have been devastated if something had happened to it. It would have been the end of my dogsled season if I did not get that sled back in one piece. With my experience of chasing these dogs, I had learned to control my fear and focus on just getting to them. Not thinking straight would only prolong finding them.

I jumped in my vehicle, drove like crazy to the next point on the trail, and listened. It was faint and traveling fast, but bells jingled faintly in the distance and kept growing louder. I knew better, but even I could have been fooled into thinking it was Christmas and Santa Claus was coming to town. Then, barreling around a bend in the trail were my dogs, pulling my sled as if it were as light as a feather, jingle bells ringing uncontrollably. I managed to stop them by making my body a human roadblock and grabbed the neckline that connected their two collars. I then placed them back into my car, went back to the start, and had a successful takeoff. I was thankful at that point to have them back safe and to have my brand-new sled back in one piece. I knew Teeka was the Houdini behind the trick because only she could mastermind an escape like that, but I also knew she ran the same trail without failing to turn off course. Teeka knew our trails right down to each turn we would take. She would even make turns sometimes without me having to tell her to. This had helped me to recover my runaway sled and dogsled team.

Although it was never her style, we have tried to force Teeka to take up couch life. Even now that she's twelve, if given the opportunity, Teeka will run away at a moment's notice. She has been the strongest and the highest strung of all of our Siberians, which is probably why she still is fully capable of leash pulling, running away, and terrorizing my parents' chickens.

The chickens had been having difficulty with critters in the night disturbing them, so my father had built a massive, beautiful wood-framed chicken coop inside the dog pen so Teeka could scare away wandering visitors. (Siberians have a prey drive, making them want to chase, capture, and kill moving objects, which in this case was the chickens. She might be older, but she has not lost her spunk.) The chicken coop was made of plywood boards, with a wooden floor and cedar siding. Teeka took it upon herself the first night the chickens and their coop joined her in the pen to "redesign" the chicken house.

She ripped off the wooden panels used as siding in her attempts to get to the chickens. Luckily, my father's design was strong enough to keep the old lady out of the coop and the chickens lived another day.

Teeka's entire demeanor changed after Rocky's passing. Our family thought she would take it very poorly. It actually turned out to be the opposite. My parents had adopted a Louisiana catahoula leopard puppy who needed a home desperately. Her name was Sophie. Sophie was adopted prior to Rocky's passing. She was a ball of fun, which was not too appealing to Rocky and Teeka in their old age. Until that point Teeka still kept to herself outside. Rocky and Sophie lived it up inside where the cookies flourished. After Rocky's passing, Teeka finally became a house-dwelling pup by choice. She would soak up living inside, sleeping on a giant dog bed made especially for her, eating cookies and special food, and allowed to get away with behaviors she had not in the past. Teeka loved her time inside. She rarely was outside from that point on.

Teeka still showed pure excitement when she saw my crew of dogs getting harnessed up. My dogs are beside themselves when they are getting ready to head out for a sled run, and Teeka was usually right there beside them. They are yipping, howling, and bouncing off the walls in anticipation. She still had high hopes that she, too, would be taken out for one last sled run. Her days of sledding were over, but she still enjoyed a long walk, dragging whoever was walking her at the other end of the leash.

I was not able to finish this story before Teeka's passing. Teeka developed cancer, and with her old age, the kind thing to do was to humanely euthanize her. She did not suffer, and she couldn't have led a better life. She is with our Rocky running to their hearts' content in the special land north of the Rainbow Bridge.

Head of State (Teeka's Story)

I knew at a very young age that I had some tidying up to do at my new home. It was a very loving and kind family that brought me into their lives. Upon arriving at my new home, I met Rocky. Rocky was quite the charmer but also a little immature for my taste. He would eventually grow on me and become the love of my life.

I needed to explore my new surroundings, but these people kept us in a closed-in area while they were away. What was I going to do, run away, maybe? You see, I get bored easily if I am not doing some form of activity. So I attempted to squirm and wiggle myself under the large, steel door that was a part of my enclosure. Well, I didn't fit, and unfortunately I experienced a lot of pain to my back leg. One of the young humans had come home and caught me under this door. He removed me safely and took me to the place that smells like a thousand animals. I met a gentleman who smelled like animals, too, but he gave me some chewable treats that helped the pain in my leg so much. I call him the animal doctor because he smelled like so many animals and because it was obvious he helped us, too. The next thing I knew, they were wrapping my leg with really heavy material and I couldn't move it at all. It actually weighed me down a lot. Well, no worries because the pain had subsided in this heavy contraption, so I figured it was okay to keep it on. After what seemed like forever lugging the heavy thing around, it came off at that animal place. The nice animal man removed it, and my leg was sore but it was free and that was all that mattered.

I liked my time alone and my space. If I wanted human contact, I would come to you. I did just fine on my own, exploring, marking my territory, and getting Rocky into -shape. Rocky was such a comic and filled my life with joy. He taught me about the land of the beepers and the zappers. I also was awarded one of the new fancy collars, which I wore with pride. I had no desire to inflict any form of pain on myself, and the land of the beepers was actually pretty far away. I wasn't sure why Rocky thought he needed to roam all that way, but hey, whatever floats your boat, buddy.

One of my people was always around and she included her canine family in her physical exercise. I loved it. I needed to run around, explore, and let my built-up energy be released. I enjoyed my time out with her so much. She would walk us almost every day for hours on end. She took it upon herself to work with me personally because I am special and beautiful. Well, actually, because I was the only one of the bunch who could comprehend what she was asking me to do.

This young girl taught me how to turn in directions that she'd request I'd turn in. I wanted to please her so much, so I made sure to do the best that I could whenever she would ask. I learned to turn a certain direction with the word "gee" and turn the other direction when she said "haw." Of course, I already knew the word *stop* because she had used it so much on our walks. I loved my days training with her. I would reach my potential and prove to be the leader she wanted.

All this training would eventually pay off for me because one day she hooked me up to a contraption with wheels that could go really fast. I wore a special harness, with special ropes attached to her wheeled thing. Then, when she was ready and I was ready, we would take off at full speed. I was running to my heart's content. There was nothing like it in the world to me. I was never happier than when I was running with my human. I listened to her every word and performed without hesitation. The more I listened, the farther we would go.

One day she took me and the wheeled contraption to a park, and we rode on the trails for hours. We would run to a lake where I could cool off, go swimming, and then we'd run again. There was nothing more thrilling and exhilarating than running. I could sense she loves it, too, because she let out big, loud sounds and her energy level was just as high as mine.

She would eventually train the rest of my canine family, but I was in charge. I let those other canines know that what I said goes. If I pushed into your shoulder, you had better go that way or I would make you sleep outside. Some nights I would have to enforce this. During my life with these people, we moved to a new house that had a large fenced-in area and an inside area for us to live in. Rocky had to find new ways to work out without his weights, but he tried very hard. The enclosure had a doggie door that led to our inside home. When the boys wouldn't listen out on a run, I'd sit by the doggie door and not allow them to come in. I had endurance and these boys knew it, so I wouldn't let up until morning. Then they could come inside.

The girl worked with me a lot out on those trails. She didn't realize that I had a map in my mind of the trails we would go on and would never get lost. One day she was having me train a new canine that had joined the family, and boy, was he clueless. All he wanted to do was run. He didn't understand that we needed to wait until she gave the command to go. His first trip out, he bolted with me attached to him, and there was no stopping that young man. So I carried on the trail like I had a thousand times before. At the bend in the trail, she was waiting and she did not seem happy. Uh-oh, I guess I should have waited for her before I took off. Well, lesson learned and next time I will stop that young man.

I kept complete control over the canines that were a part of my family. Listening to my people was gratifying and rewarding to me. The girl took me out running on so many occasions with or without snow. I learned to lead the male canines in my life with pride and joy.

Rocky fell very ill one day, and he would not even accept the cookies that he so loved. We were inside our people's house sleeping through the night. He woke up feeling better, and we went about our lives like normal. I was taking an afternoon nap, and when I awoke, I went to check on him. When I saw him, I knew. He had gone on to that special place for us that we all look forward to going someday. I lay beside him, letting my soul mourn the loss of the only love that I had ever known. I could only imagine how different life would be without him. My people finally arrived home and also came to our living area to check on him. The tall man fell to his knees and began to weep. I could sense he was very upset at seeing Rocky. He wrapped him up in a blanket and removed him from our area. I was welcomed into the house, where the people hugged me and cried into my hair. Death can be so devastating, even for the people who care for us. I loved Rocky with all my heart, but I know that I will see him again someday.

Panda

Just one look at Panda and you will understand how he got his name. Panda is the first pup we kept from a litter that Rocky and Teeka had. The entire litter was filled with all red-colored puppies. Panda was a long-haired red baby boy whose personality came mostly from his mother, Teeka. My oldest brother, Adam, had decided to keep him for his own. Adam has never been a musher, but he wanted to own a dog of his own as a pet. Panda grew into a ninety-pound long-haired mammoth. To this day he still carries his long hair, bright, piercing blue eyes, and kind demeanor. He is the gentlest natured out of all of my puppies. Panda also is currently in retirement; at the age of eleven, his large size cannot handle the arthritis that has set into his joints. However, that does not stop him from long summer morning walks to go swimming in the lakes and rivers close by. In the winter Panda runs alongside the sled until he reaches his stopping point, where he then jumps on the sled and the rest of the crew proceeds to pull him along, much to their dismay. Panda is still very outgoing and not letting his old age slow him down.

Panda was our first of this breed to not run away if he was off the leash. Adam would always let Panda out to roam the yard and do as he pleased. When Adam went off to college, Panda remained at our parents' house with his parents, Rocky and Teeka. Anytime Adam was around, Panda knew that he was his, and soon he would be let out to enjoy time with him. His sweet nature made him unique and special to anyone who met him. Panda remained well-mannered and obedient until our second litter of puppies came around and I chose to keep a little male puppy named Toby.

There was a time when Panda participated in whatever Toby did. One evening in the middle of winter while freezing rain fell, Toby and Panda decided to go for a stroll. This particular time I had a rental car; it was a Taurus and was not a well-equipped snow vehicle. I was used to driving a four-wheel drive SUV, so this Taurus took some getting used to. I began to look for the dogs, but I was not able to identify the route they had taken. At that moment I realized my search could only go so far because my gas tank was getting close to empty. I searched for about five hours around the ski resort and then decided to head into town to see if there was a twenty-four-hour gas station.

On the route I had to take, I knew there was one particular hill that was sure to cause me some trouble. It was about a quarter of a mile long and at a forty-five-degree angle. I slowly began down the hill using the side of the road to grab the tires where the dirt was still showing. I began picking up speed and continued to brake check, but I was not able to slow down. At the end of the long hill was a very sharp curve to the right, and a small house sat just the opposite side of the road. I was losing control of the car as I drove toward this house, white-knuckling the steering wheel. Luckily enough I managed to swipe through their front yard and miss the house.

"No, Officer, I was not drinking. I am searching at 4 a.m. for my two lost dogs." How was I going to explain at four in the morning, why I had crashed into a house looking for my lost dogs? No injury to car, no injury to house, so I continued on with my pursuit, hoping nobody was awake to witness that.

When I reached the town, the gas light in the car came on, but there were no twenty-four-hour gas stations. I went back home because I had to teach snowboard lessons in the morning and I needed gas to get there. I reached home around five with no sign of the dogs. I waited and looked around the house until I had to head in to work. It was difficult to concentrate with my sleep deprivation and anxiety over where the dogs could be. It wasn't long after my first lesson began that I noticed a police officer walking down the pathway to where I was.

As he got closer, I could tell he was looking in my direction. When he asked if I was the owner of Panda and Toby, I felt my heart sink to my feet. I reluctantly answered yes. He said that he had them in the squad car out front. Thank goodness for ID tags and leaving messages all night long at Animal control. He assured me they were alright but very tired. I apologized to my students and went to collect my dogs.

Sure enough, there were Toby and Panda sitting in the back of a police squad car. He said they were found in front of the police station going from bush to bush and letting the neighborhood dogs know they had been there. I thanked him ever so much, placed them in my car, and finished my lesson. When the lesson was over, I quickly drove them home. It was the first time that my dogs had ever been in a police car. I had never even been in the back of a police car myself before! Not that I want to, but I would have never guessed my dogs would. Let's hope that is the one and only time that happens.

I'm Not a Lion (Panda's Story)

I grew up with my people and my parents, Rocky and Teeka. I am a laid-back, easygoing dog that lets life roll on by. Whatever is thrown at me, I take it with a grain of salt. My life is filled with love and joy from a young boy who takes me almost everywhere he goes. When he is not around, the young girl takes me for walks and allows me to go running with my parents. This girl also takes me to Dogville, and it is such an amazing place to go.

At Dogville I can run around and be crazy with my other canine friends. There are pools, toys, and things to climb at this place. All the canines are so happy to be there so everyone gets along.

There is only person to be afraid of at Dogville, and she has fire in her hair. She can capture you and force you to be sprayed with water. I then have this flower-like smell lathered all over me and am forced to sit in it for, like, a day. Okay, not an entire day, but it felt like it. Once I am done sitting in the flowery stuff, I get sprayed with water all over again. Look, lady, if I wanted to play in the water, I could have easily done it in the pools outside with my friends where it is a lot more fun. When the water spraying is done, I get blasted by a stream of air. It blows my hair all over, making me look like a lion, but I am not a lion, people!

The people in my life take me many places, especially the girl. She has introduced me to many canines over the years, and I am sure to let them know that I have been here a long time and they need to stay in line. Over the years my bones began to creak and throb. They just weren't like they used to be. The girl feeds me lots of goodies that make the pain go away. I know what time of day I get them, so I just take myself into the kitchen and bark to let her know I am there in case she forgot. Then for the rest of the day I just want to eat, eat, eat. I don't know what it is, but I can run around like a crazy person and eat like a horse. I feel great and can move so much easier after that. I feel so much better and the pain I was having before she started giving me all the snacks has subsided.

I love the life that I live. The girl who lives with me lets me lounge on the couches. I can go in and out of the house as I please. I get to go swimming, meet other new dogs, and see lots of new people, too. There are a lot of people out there who find me fascinating, but I am not sure why. Must be the hair—I should have been a model. Yes, I run in a line with a bunch of dogs pulling my person around, and other people just love it. I live a great life, and I wouldn't trade it for anything.

Toby

Toby was that special dog that comes along and touches your heart so deeply- that you feel no other dog is ever going to compare. Toby was from -an "oops" litter of puppies we had from Rocky and Teeka. We had intended on spaying Teeka after her first litter of puppies, but she came into heat quicker than we had anticipated. We had kept Rocky and Teeka separate, but one day, our little Rocky chewed through a chain-link fence and Toby was the end result. This litter of puppies was a mixture of traditional red and white Siberian and malamute breeds. Toby was the biggest puppy of the litter and the first one to be born. Teeka had a very difficult time delivering him due to his large body size. Toby was a black and white, long-haired bi-eyed puppy. (Bi-eyed means he had two different-colored eyes.)

I had no intention of keeping Toby until he was one of the last puppies left. But s-ecretly, when people came to look at the puppies I would hide him. My poor parents didn't catch on until he was the only one left. They couldn't figure out why he was still there. Everyone always wanted the larger of the puppies. But with a lot of begging and pleading, Toby became mine.

Toby would turn into a very large troublemaker. He was smart and always on his toes. He could always find a way out of any enclosure he was in. Toby and I soon became inseparable. He would travel to soccer games, pet stores, and vacation trips up north; everywhere I would go, he would come along. I soon realized Toby was a very special and cunning young boy. He was as gentle-natured as his older brother Panda, always loving to strangers, and never showed an aggressive bone in his body. As he got older, his stunts would begin to take place, just like what happened with his father, Rocky.

During the summer months, I lived in Bellaire, Michigan, with Toby, Panda, and my brother. So Toby and Panda got to live together with us while we worked at the local golf courses. We worked at two of the resort's golf courses, sometimes on different shifts. One afternoon we both came home to find that the two of them had escaped. We went looking all over the resort for them. We had put special calls out to the rangers patrolling the four courses to keep an eye out for them. After hours of looking, a ranger finally spotted them on the eighteenth green of one of the courses. They were holding up play. Panda has always hated water, but Toby loved it. Surrounding the green was a very large pond with a great amount of Canadian geese. Toby was completely submerged with only his head above water. He was swimming in the water as smooth as a crocodile, chasing the geese in every direction while Panda waited on the shoreline. Panda would attempt to go in the water, going as far in as he could until the water touched his belly, then out he came. Panda had four green, pond-scum-covered legs that looked as if he were wearing boots on each leg by the time they were done.

Thankfully, they did not find success in these antics and the geese lived another day. When we retrieved them, they exuded a smell only a stagnant pond in ninety-degree heat could emit. They were covered in the dark green, slimy pond scum and even a few pieces of seaweed. We placed them in our car, windows rolled all the way down, and headed home for a bath. Toby and Panda did not score a birdie that day, but they definitely played the entire hole. Golf play resumed, and thankfully that was their only golfing experience.

Toby was mischievous. He could cause trouble at the drop of a hat. One evening my brother made a wonderful batch of enchiladas for dinner. Cooking was a new adventure for my brother and me, so he was pretty impressed with his tasty dinner. We left them on the counter to cool and walked away. Toby was around two years old. He had never been one to steal food off a counter before. My brother and

I both became occupied with something and turned our backs on the food. Toby saw his opportunity, and before we knew it, our dinner was gone and the plate was licked clean. It was as if the dish was fresh out of the dishwasher, no stains either! Toby, however, had grown a large, red-stained mustache across his face that I am positive was not there before. His lesson was learned quickly when his stomach disagreed with his choice of food for dinner.

Toby and Panda were inseparable. Wherever Toby went, Panda followed. In the winter one year, Toby and Panda escaped again at the ski resort. We searched all over the mountain and alerted the ski patrol we were looking for them. Soon we received a call that they had been found at a hotel on the grounds. I drove over to the hotel, and as I entered, I asked the concierge where the two Siberians had been found. As a large smile crossed her face, I looked down and at her feet there were Toby and Panda.

She informed me that while they were on their winter excursion, they'd crossed in front of the large, brand-new hotel with automatic doors that entered into the lobby. I am sure motion-sensing technology was not designed to keep from opening when runaway ninety-pound dogs pass by, so they were able to walk right in.

As they entered, the smells of Italian food filled their nostrils and led them right into a restaurant, where they went from table to table begging for food. The tables had white linen seat covers, with white linen table covers, and the finest silverware available. I was mortified; I grabbed them quickly and escorted them out to my car. The people in the restaurant loved them, though, and thankfully found it funny. I mean, how often do you visit a five-star hotel restaurant and end up having two very large stray dogs wander up to your table begging for food? I was sure that their trips to the hotel were over, but they would quickly prove me wrong.

A couple of weeks later, we returned to the mountain for more skiing. We did not have a fenced-in area at the cabin because they were not allowed on the resort property. The two boys were kept on tie outs when they went outside. It didn't take long after we left for the two of them to get loose and make a break for it again. Back to the hotel they went. I set out in my car searching and searching for them. I got another phone call from the hotel while I was out looking, telling me that they had made a return visit.

As I went to pick them up, I found a surprise. Our dogs have always been sociable, and apparently they did not want their friends to miss out on the fun, as well. This time behind the concierge desk were Toby, Panda, and two black labs, all of which had passed through the motion-sensing doors, entered the hotel, and gone into the restaurant. I was so embarrassed. They handed me back our dogs, and I politely said how sorry I was they had come back. I again gathered my dogs and headed back home. Toby was always the instigator with the antics those two played; nevertheless, he has always held that special place in my heart.

As I mentioned before, Toby was an escape artist. If he was left alone, he would begin to plot how get out of his enclosure. I remember one day I came home from work and Toby was running free in the front yard. He was giving me that look like, "Where have you been all day?" I could not figure out how he had escaped: the fencing was intact, and the main door to the barn and the kennel were closed. As I approached the barn door, I realized this time that the screen in the window was torn. I then put it together and realized Toby had escaped through the window.

Now to figure out how he got out of the ten-foot-high chain-link fence in the barn was my next challenge. I placed Toby back in the kennel and hid in the barn to observe his escape tactics. In the indoor portion of the kennel we had a green La-Z-Boy chair for them to sit in. It was then I realized the chair had been pushed into the corner of the kennel in alignment with my father's workbench. A theory was developing in my head of how Toby had performed this escape.

Toby began to act anxious and started to pace back and forth. Slowly he went to the green La-Z-Boy recliner. He ever so slowly eased himself up on it, as if he was thinking someone was watching and he would get in trouble. Toby would then climb the fence, land on the workbench on the other side, get down, go to the window, and use his nose to lift it open and proceed to climb out. The chair in the kennel had to be removed and the window had to be locked. Toby never did get out of the kennel again.

His escape antics helped me to understand his intelligence. If he was capable of figuring out all of these escape routes, then he was smart enough to train as a lead dog. I began to partner him with his mom, Teeka. It only took a couple of days for him to understand the commands. And if he didn't get them, Teeka was sure to remind him to turn right or left.

Out of all of my dogs, Toby was very special to me. He was the first dog I owned, and he was a huge part of my life. One morning I was going to the daycare I worked for, and I had Toby, Panda, and Rocky with me. I was the first to arrive at work. As I went to get the dogs out and enter the building, they got loose from the car and took off after a rabbit. The building was a ways off the road, but still it was a very busy road. The dogs attempted to cross the traffic in pursuit of the rabbit, but Toby didn't make it. I was in my car, racing down the drive. When I got into the road, it was then my heart stopped. I could see a SUV stopped and Toby lying motionless in the road. He was still alive, but my first thoughts were of getting Panda and Rocky into the car to remove them from danger, and then get Toby.

I quickly grabbed Rocky and Panda and placed them in the car before they were harmed. The driver of the other vehicle assisted me in placing Toby in my car. A vet was a few miles down the road, and I was going to do everything I could to get him there. He was still alive when he was placed in the car, and I took off. In about five minutes I arrived, although it seemed like forever. I ran to the door, pounding and screaming for someone to help me. It was before clinic hours, and I was instructed to go across town to the emergency clinic. I knew he couldn't make it that far, and I think the poor girl heard the plea in my voice. The vet tech ran outside with me to my car, when I opened the car door I knew…he was gone. But

She listened with her stethoscope, and it was then I realized things were never going to be the same. My life had changed so much in a matter of minutes. Toby looked just like he was sleeping and that he should wake up. I knew the injuries were deeper than I could see.

I felt numb, I couldn't cry, I just sank to the ground. What was I going to do without him? How could I ever love another dog like him? I lost my best friend that day on the road, and I feared I would never have that bond again.

It's at hard times like this that you need to rely on your family and friends. We took Toby back home and we all said our good-byes. Toby was laid to rest that day under a beautiful weeping cherry tree outside my bedroom window, wrapped in his favorite blanket and with his favorite toy. He took his place at the Rainbow Bridge, and I know that he is having the time of his life just waiting for me to return to him.

My thoughts raced for months after. How could he leave me? What was I going to do? How was he going to be without me? I just needed reassurance that he was somewhere that he didn't look for me, that he didn't need me anymore, and that he was safe. I kept replaying the accident in my head for days following. Could I have done something different? It was my own self-induced torture that replayed like a movie in my mind. All the pictures of him were removed from my room. My bedding was stripped because his hair was on it. I slept in the living room with a new comforter because it didn't remind me of him. I couldn't even drive my own car for weeks because the memories were too strong. My mother let me borrow hers. But time heals everything, and it did. It just took a little longer for me than I expected.

I want everyone to know that yes, when you lose a pet you think you can't move on and that you won't love another the same way. I want to say that's true. You won't love another pet the same way, but you will love a new pet in a special way that's just for them.

You never truly get over something like that. It replays over and over in your head like a movie on repeat. The images of him going down in the road would not stop. I had to find other things to try to occupy myself. Luckily, at that time I had a very sick puppy that needed my help. It turned out we both helped each other.

The Easy Life (Toby's Story)

I was born into a life of luxury and love. Growing up in the younger years of my life with my brothers and sisters was a memorable time. There was a little girl who played for hours with my brothers, sisters, and me. We would chase her all over the front lawn, pull on her clothes, and give her puppy kisses. She was a lot of fun and kept us tired.

I remember there were people who would come to see my family and me. One by one my siblings would go home with these wonderful people. The little girl would constantly hide me away from them when people would come. I wanted to meet these people, too. Eventually, I was the only puppy left, and I was sad. Why had she hidden me all the time? I was never going to find a family of my own. Then one day she came to me and put a collar on me. It was then I knew. She was hiding me because she wanted to keep me. I had a family! The girl was keeping me for her very own, and I could stay with my big brother and parents. Life was going to be good.

I would go everywhere with the girl. She would take me to get delicious, frozen snacks, and watch kids kick a ball around the grass. I would get to share her bed with her every night. I took up most of the room, but she didn't mind. I also got to go to Dogville with Rocky and Panda. The dogs I got to meet there were amazing. They all wanted to play with me, too. We were inseparable, the two of us.

Panda had warned me about the girl with fire in her hair. She would come and get you and take you through a secret door to the land of flowers. We called it that because it smelled like flowers in there. She would put me in an area and splash water on me. I would start to cry and cry because it was so awful. I was getting all wet. The only time I would not cry was when my girl splashed the water on me. If my girl was doing it, I didn't mind, but if it was the girl with fire in her hair, all bets were off. I became a howling madman. My hopes were that my sounds would be so awful that she would stop. The next thing I knew, she put big puffy things on her ears that I am pretty sure were designed to drown me out. Tricky, tricky, tricky, lady.

I grew attached to the girl and needed to be wherever she was whenever I could. The many tactics and diversions I came up with were astounding. I could climb the highest fence, open any window, and jump through screens to get to her. She was my everything, and I needed to be by her. One day she brought home a special collar that smelled very pleasant. It created a calming feeling for me, and my desire to escape to get to her lessened. She was clever, but over time the calming scent wore away and I was back at it. I have to give her credit for trying. Good effort on her part. Pheromone collars, ha! Who did she think she was?

As I grew older, I realized that Panda was my best bud. He and I would do everything together when my girl wasn't around. I had a genius idea one day to run around and see what we could find. Panda was never too keen on taking off, but I was excellent at persuasion. An adventure I remember so well was when we found all these birds swimming around a water hole. Panda never liked getting wet, so he stayed on the shoreline while I swam after the feathered creatures. I was an excellent swimmer and was able to gain ground on them. While swimming, I attempted to make the feathered creatures go toward Panda, who was waiting. Those things had a surprise for me that I did not see coming: they could fly! They would take off before Panda ever had a chance. It was all about the chase and the hunt, though. Our fun ended when my girl came and found us. She made us go home with her, and then we got sprayed with water. To make matters worse, she put flower-smelling stuff on us. The fire-haired lady had given her some, oh boy. How embarrassing is that?

The best time of my life was when she would take my parents, my brother, and me out to go running. It was the thrill of a lifetime. I got to run lead with my mom, Teeka. Teeka was so smart and skilled at what she did. She would teach me something new every time we went out. I learned how to listen to the girl when she would say certain commands. I must say that I got pretty good at it. We would take trips to new locations, and we could go running until we could no longer run. It was a moment in my life that I would never forget.

Okay, I admit I was a bad influence on my brother, Panda, but I just wanted to have fun. One evening I decided to get us out of the fenced-in area where we were and go exploring. It was winter, which was the best time to run because we would not overheat. Once we escaped we went to the land of gliding giants. They were people who glided on the snow, up and down hills. Once they glided to the bottom, they rode large, metal machines back to the top of the hill. I didn't quite understand it, but I thought, oh well, at least they enjoy it like me when I'm running.

We were romping through the snow, having the time of our lives, and I lost track of time. It grew dark and a storm was coming. The freezing rain began to set in, and I knew we needed to head home, but we had accidently wandered very far away. Panda and I decided to stay put until the storm was over and then head home in the morning. When morning came, a gentleman was standing over us. He put leashes on us and placed us in his car. I was nervous. What if he didn't take us back to our girl? Would she ever find us? Fear began to set in. He drove us around for a while and finally took us to a big, tall building. The next thing I knew, my girl was there. I was so happy to see her and I think she was with me, too. She grabbed me so tightly and cried. I knew then that what I had done had hurt her feelings. It was so hard to not want to run, though. It was a burning urge that was always around telling me to run, run, run.

I loved spending every waking moment with my girl and running. She was good at making sure I was able to run with her and my family most of the time. I loved snuggling with her, getting all the special treats she would have for me, and most of all just being around her. I tried to please her in any way that I could and made sure I gave her lots of kisses. I had a life on easy street; what's not to love about that?

Learning to Run

It was while I worked at the doggie daycare that I found my passion for dogs. It was a large facility that dogs came to every day to be watched while their owners were at work. How lucky was I to be able to take my dogs with me to work? During my time there, I realized what responsible dog owners did with their dogs. They had them groomed, learned about what foods seemed good but really were not, and most of all exercised them. I realized then that most of their behavioral problems had been due to failure to properly exercise my dogs. So I began to walk my dogs every day. I began to understand that was a very complicated task. They pulled on their leashes like they were running the Iditarod. My own strength would only allow me to walk two at a time safely. But I did not have two hours of time in each of my days to reserve for walking the dogs since I had to split them up. I would walk each group for an hour every day.

I had to find another way to walk them all at once. Dogsledding came to mind. I knew absolutely nothing about it, nor did I know anyone who did it at the time. I had walking harnesses for all of them, leashes, and a mountain bike. Not the best idea, I know, but I had to try something. My first dogsledding trip down the driveway on my mountain bike with just two dogs was out of control. They were running at lightning speed, and I was holding on for dear life. I understood then that I had the wrong style harnesses, the wrong equipment, and I needed to do some research.

This first run down the driveway was so exhilarating and amazing that I knew I had to pursue this hobby even further. I knew I had to train the dogs to turn, stop, and obey me when I was a distance behind them. There was equipment that I was going to have to purchase—like a sled and lines—to make this even more fun. That first run on the bike down the driveway created a desire for dogsledding that grew into a huge part of my life.

I had no experience with training dogs. Deciding how to train a lead dog was a challenge for me. I decided to work with Teeka, and began to teach her left and right commands. I used a training lead and worked with right turn commands for a week. She would walk in front of me and I would say "gee." When she made the turn, I would reward her with a treat. Once she learned "gee," we moved on to "haw," which means to turn left. Using the same techniques, she learned both commands. Whether this was the correct way of training or not, it worked.

Teeka and I then started training together on the bike. I lived next to a state park that happened to be vacant because it was early spring and they were not open yet. By then I had purchased the correct X-back harnesses and lines used for dogsledding, and she was harnessed to the bike. The two of us worked for a week straight, making right hand turns only through the park. When she had mastered the command to turn right, we worked for the following week turning left. Teeka was able to make both turns beautifully with minimal hesitation. It was then that I had the confidence in her to hook up the other dogs.

The problem I faced then was that the other dogs did not how to stop, turn, slow down, or stay…big problem! Teeka was not proving strong enough to keep the other dogs in line. Hooking all four dogs up to the mountain bike proved to be an extremely scary experience. I was flying out of control, down the driveway with a group of dogs that wanted to run in all different directions. I needed to strategize again. These pups needed weight and a brake system to slow them down so they could learn as a team. Our John Deere riding lawn mower popped into my mind!

It had a lot weight and a brake system that I knew could hold those four dogs. I am sure I looked like the hillbilly dog sled team from the country but it worked like a charm. We had a long driveway made of dirt, with lots of trees surrounding us, and I trained them up and down the driveway all the time. They soon became very well behaved with stopping and turning. They would run full-tilt down the driveway and turn around so fast I would barely have time to adjust. Toby and Teeka became my lead dogs, while Panda and Rocky were trained to be wheel dogs.

The dogs and I learned the art of dogsledding together. We learned to face new challenges together, devising strategies to overcome them. It was like the game of life. You take whatever is dealt and learn to get through it safely. We learned that I needed to teach a command to have them leave something alone. So I use "on by" to keep them moving on a trail away from a distraction. There were times when we were traveling way too fast and I just needed to slow them down, not stop them but slow them down. So I used the word "easy" and applied the brakes. This was a pretty smart group of pups, and it didn't take them long to catch on to the new lingo I was throwing at them.

My work schedule didn't allow me to get runs in some days because it grew dark before I could get home. This did not stop me. I used a flashlight that I duct-taped to the handlebars on my bike. After weeks of using my hillbilly design, I was educated on a useful item called a headlamp. It was so much easier to use than a flashlight and duct tape, I must say.

The driveway soon became boring and we needed to venture to longer trails. A state park was located one half mile from my parents' house with endless miles of trails. Soon we learned to run these trails with help from a well-trained Teeka. She would push Toby to follow the commands I was giving. Teeka was excellent at dropping her shoulder into Toby's rib area to guide him at turns. Teeka would soon prove to be a caliber of lead dog you come across once in a lifetime. It was amazing how the runaway attempts and behavioral antics we'd had prior to sledding all began to decrease at drastic rates. That did not mean they still would not have more tricks up their sleeves, though.

After a summer of training, I decided to buy a dogsled in the fall. I researched and found a local gentleman who made wooden sleds strong enough to handle my four crazy sled pups. The sled was beautiful with a glossy wood shine, rawhide handlebars, and large snow hook, which I soon would realize was my saving grace, and a large claw brake system to stop them. The sled was remarkable.

I could not wait for the first snow to come so I could have my chance to dogsled for real. It wasn't long after I purchased the sled that the snow began to fall. I kept the dogs running with the mountain bike until the snow began to blanket the ground, and then the chance of slipping became too much and the bike was stored for the winter.

It seemed like forever waiting for the snow to become deep enough to take the sled out. When the snow finally arrived and I took the team out for our first run, it was like learning all over again. The sled moves in a way that only a musher can describe. I feel I have earned the title of a "musher" by now. I have been bruised, scratched, thrown, and pulled at high speeds behind a team of high-energy Siberians. I have somehow managed to train a team of four dogs without having a clue what I was doing. But I have a dogsled team and I am a musher.

The sled moves with you, the dogs, and your body weight. You need to learn to adjust the 1speed for corners, so you do not dump the sled (which happened often). The dogs were very well trained at that point, and they were easy to command while I learned to understand the motions of the sled. The more I was on the sled, the more tricks I learned to move it around the trail. If I dropped my foot off the side of the sled, I could make sharper corners. I would put my weight on one runner of the sled to push it in one direction without going around a corner. (A runner is the two pieces of wood that come off the back of sled for the musher to stand on.)

We ran every weekend in the winter at the ski resort by our family's cabin, and I also ran them on the trails back home. The amount of energy they give when running in the winter compared to the summer is entirely different. The high-pitched barking, the whining, the jumping, the restlessness in anticipation for the run to start is what sledding is all about. The dogs run because they love it. I am often asked if the dogs enjoy it or if they are doing it because they are expected to. To answer this I simply say, the only way I can anchor them at the start is to my Ford F-150 truck. If they aren't tied to that, they would be gone. They also jump up and down in their harnesses while attached to the lines waiting to go. The dogs bark, whine, and yelp, and some I would say scream in anticipation waiting for me to release them to run. It is in their blood and their heritage. They have an unimaginable ability to run for long distances and still have the endurance and drive to want to keep going every day. I still sled today, but it is only for the pure enjoyment of the sport. To find time when you can step away from the world and enjoy a trail ride through nature's own paradise is the opportunity of a lifetime.

There are many different ways to raise a dogsled team. I selected the "treating-them-as- household-pets" lifestyle, but that is not the most common way of life for sled dogs. Most dogsled teams that participate for sport are kenneled outside and to a specific length of chain attached to a doghouse or barrel used for shelter. The chains are kept at a minimal distance to prevent tangling with the other dogs. They have access to water, food, and shelter. Keep in mind, these dogs are exercised daily, for long distances. They take a lot of time to recuperate when done. So a small living area for these dogs does not bother them, and the dogs are used to this way of life simply because they do not know any differently. Sled dogs can live a more fulfilled life than most house pets. Sled dog owners are very responsible with their dogs, watching their diet, adjusting calorie needs, exercising, providing fresh water and food, and cleaning up after their dogs so they do not live in filth.

There is no right or wrong way to learn how to dogsled. As long as the dogs have water, food, shelter, exercise, and love, they will have a happy life. Many dogs from kennels go up for adoption once they reach retirement age. Retirement can happen at a young age for sled dogs on professional teams because they mainly run with younger dogs. This is a great way to adopt one of these dogs because you can still have a long life with your four-legged companion.

Kodah

Kodah is a unique and special little boy that came into my life when I needed him the most. Remember that sick little puppy I had to take care of? That was my little Kodah. He is an Alaskan malamute and Siberian husky mix. I got him when he was about three months old from a dogsledder who owned many dogs. Kodah was from a litter of puppies that he was selling and had no use for. I made a long three-hour car ride with my mom to get Kodah. Kodah had a long silver and black body with a bright orange head. He was not the most attractive puppy, but for some strange reason I was drawn to him. I picked him up on a Thursday night, and we drove him home.

I decided to add Kodah to my life because I wanted to own another dog, especially since dogsledding was proving to be the thrill of my life. I wanted to add to my dogsled team. My team was still young and learning, but so was I. I had been sledding for about a year when I decided to get Kodah.

At that time, I still had Toby with me. Kodah was the second dog I ever owned. The following day I had nursing clinicals at the hospital, and so I left him in the care of my mother. She called me after clinicals and said he had been throwing up all day and not eating. When I arrived home, he was not his usual self. As the evening went on, he began to get worse. We contacted our vet at home and he said to bring him in the first thing in the morning. We drove him in on a Saturday morning, and they performed the PARVO test, which came back with a strong positive. PARVO is a virus that young dogs tend to be more susceptible to. This virus is highly contagious, is transmitted through fecal material, and attacks the dog's intestinal tract. Kodah presented with lethargy, no appetite, uncontrolled diarrhea, and vomiting. Kodah had a life-threatening viral disease that usually did not have a positive outcome.

This could have been prevented by simple vaccinations that the prior owner did not administer. Puppies go through a series of vaccines that help them build immunity to illnesses like the PARVO virus. Kodah wasn't given much hope to survive, but I wanted to try. By the beginning of the next week, he was still hanging in there. He was weak, not eating, receiving IV fluids, and had high temperatures. On Tuesday when I called the vet, they said he was not doing well, his fever had spiked, he was lethargic, and I would need to start thinking about humanely euthanizing him. I thought over it that night for a long time. The next day I was going to go to see Kodah and make the decision, but that was also the morning of Toby's accident and I was not able to make that painful decision. It was too much for me in one day. I felt lost after Toby's passing, but I still wanted to go see Kodah. I drove straight from the vet where Toby had been taken to my vet where Kodah was.

Seeing Kodah I somehow thought he would ease the pain I was feeling from losing Toby. The vet was kind enough to place him in a private room for me to visit him. Kodah did not know me at all, because most of the time I had owned him he had been at the vet. But when he entered the room, I was sitting on the floor and he made a straight line for me and curled up in my lap. It was as if he knew how much I was hurting and just wanted to provide comfort. Kodah had shown a lot of improvement that day, and the vet said there was a possibility I could take him home soon. He also told me Kodah was the only PARVO puppy he had that year to survive.

Deep down I knew it was because there was a special dog looking over him, making sure Kodah came back home with me. Kodah would begin to grow and carry on a lot of the personality traits that were so similar to Toby. There are mysterious acts in this world that sometimes we cannot explain. I felt like somehow someone was ensuring he stayed with me because Toby was taken too soon and they were saying, "I'm sorry, but I'm giving you Kodah."

Kodah was able to come home with me two days after Toby's passing. During his recovery time, Kodah was developing strange tastes for food. His gastrointestinal tract was still not up to par yet, and he needed frequent bathroom trips outside. One day, Kodah got into a large packet of suet birdseed that my mother had in the garage. So among his many trips outside, he now was depositing sunflower seeds all over the yard. Over the next few weeks, large sunflower plants began to sprout in many areas of our lawn. Kodah had left his calling card all over the yard that my parents had worked so hard to keep lush and green. I do recall my mother not being pleased.

Kodah has been full of life and joy since the day I got him. He is a mischievous little pup with the sweetest of souls. Kodah is aware that he still holds a special place in my heart and that he can get away with a lot of things that I don't necessarily allow the other pups to do. If you are sitting on the floor, his favorite thing to do is to come over and sit on you. He will do it to anyone of any age or size. At the dog bakery in town, an employee came to give him a treat and he sat on the floor near Kodah. Kodah just turned his body and sat on him. Then he proceeded to turn his head, looking back at the man whom he was sitting on, to look for the cookie he was to receive. He sat there so proud, the corners of his mouth drawn back, so that you would think he was smiling.

I do know this is a form of dominance being exhibited by him, but I cannot help but just laugh when this hundred-and-fifteen-pound dog sits on people. Sorry, Dog Whisperer, I will do better in the future.

Kodah is a people lover. Anywhere he goes he loves the attention that people give him. Kodah has a natural smile that spreads across his face when he is happy. Kodah is great with people, children, and all animals that he comes across. His gentle nature and big heart make him so loving to all the people who get the opportunity to meet him.

The other talent that Kodah has is the "whoo whoo" that he does in public when he is around people. Unfortunately, his voice loves to make its appearance in quiet situations. It does draw people to him and then he gets what he wants…attention. The worst place to take a bellowing dog is to a warehouse pet supply store. It is amazing the echo he can produce off the walls in those places. Imagine standing in an enclosed room with about ten cell phones ringing at once. That is Kodah in a warehouse.

Kodah also has that innate Siberian husky instinct to run, as well. One evening my father was repairing their kennel and Kodah escaped. Even he, being one of my best behaved dogs, took advantage of the gate being unlocked to the fenced-in yard. I was working the night shift at this time. My father looked everywhere for him with the help of one of my neighbors. He eventually got a hold of me after hours of searching to inform me that Kodah was lost. After the panic began to subside, I realized that I had gone swimming with him earlier in the day and his collar was off drying, therefore he had no contact information on him. Yeah, that panic that had subsided swept over me all over again, taking my breath away. Out of all my dogs, why did it have to be Kodah?

I live two blocks away from an ice cream store, and after searching for hours, my father stopped and asked if they had seen him. The employee said yes, he had made quite a bit of money off my dog. Kodah had stopped by and hung around for a couple of hours while people purchased him ice cream. I can imagine this scene in my mind. Kodah's overzealous attitude would draw people to him, he would do his usual bellow, stare at their ice cream, and bellow again until they gave him some. He would run with excitement to each new arriving customer and follow them to the counter. I am sure the staff gave them the wonderful suggestion of buying him ice cream and sure enough he would receive more. My poor father must have passed by so many times but never realized he was there. When the people had dispersed, Kodah just left and meandered on his way.

My father eventually did find him that evening, but quite a distance away from my house. Kodah was found about six miles away at someone's house who luckily had encountered my father out looking for him and took his number. I learned a very important lesson that day. I now have swimming collars and house collars. My dogs have never been without identification tags since. I am sure other dog owners understand that you learn from your dogs. Mistakes happen, and that is life. Unfortunately our society is becoming more of a "one strike and you're out" environment for our canine companions. My hope is that one day fewer and fewer animal shelters and humane societies will be needed. Animals should be given that second opportunity for life and have a home to go to.

Kodah is the tallest of all the dogs. He is a large and, most of the time, lazy ball of fur. While he is very capable of climbing onto many of the surfaces that he wishes, he will put his two front feet up and then look back with that idiotic smile on his face, asking, "Are you going to help or what?" I have captured video of this act, and when he gets frustrated at me for not helping, the whoo-whoos start to roar out of that little mouth of his. The only object that does not seem to cause a problem for him to jump onto is the couch. Kodah can lie there for hours, and he requires no help from me to get there. Over the years Kodah has learned that I pretty much let him get away with…well, just about anything.

One day, I was to meet my family at my grandfather's farm, which is also home to many cows that roam the property. This was when Kodah was actually behaving off the leash and would listen to commands I would give him. When we arrived, I let my dogs out to have a break from riding in the car. Kodah was let off the leash with the remaining dogs still on the leash. Once he was out and made his pass through the lawn, suddenly he caught sight of the cows down by the river. Now, in my mind I thought, *Why in the world would he even mess with an animal that is triple his size.*

He took off down into the pasture and began to chase the cattle around. I called and called, but he refused to listen to me, so I made my way down through the mucky, swampy pasture to get to the area of land where the cattle were grazing. My mother had not been aware of the activities taking place and was in the house. There were only about eight or nine cows in the field and Kodah was whoo-whooing, chasing them around and bouncing around like he didn't have a care in the world.

Once I got closer, Kodah did come to me, but it was then that I heard my mother in the distance. Her voice was panicked and she yelled, "Those are bulls!" At that time, the bulls had already begun to charge Kodah, and we were barely managing to just stay out of their range. I quickly grabbed Kodah, and we made a run for it. We took off splashing through the "mud" I had worked so hard to avoid. We finally made it out of the pasture safely, but we were both completely covered in smelly, thick, black swamp muck, which I am sure was really a combination of mud and manure. We hosed ourselves off, but the smell that lingered on him for the car ride home was enough to keep the windows rolled down the entire trip.

Kodah has always had the attitude of *I know that I am the chosen one and I am going to use that to my advantage.* When I'm sleeping, he loves to sneak up on the bed. I wake up simply because I find myself not having room to roll over. When I look for the culprit, I find that Kodah has occupied most of the middle of the bed, lying with all four feet in the air, jowls hanging loose to the bed, and tongue sticking out to one side. My only thought is, *I sure hope he is comfortable because it's not going to last long.* With that thought I roll his large body over. Why is it that dogs think they can just occupy any comfy, plush surface and make it theirs?

One day, I was preparing the sled and the dogs to take off for a run. I had the sled loaded on the roof rack of my SUV and the dogs loaded in the car. I then realized I'd forgotten my gloves in the house. I left the dogs in the truck and went into the house to collect them. When I returned to the car, what I saw had me laughing so hard I almost fell over. Kodah was sitting in the driver's seat behind the steering wheel and Rocky had placed himself in the passenger's seat. I had to do a double-take because behind them peering around the seats sat Teeka and Panda. I kept laughing hysterically because the sled was in perfect position on top of the car and it made the dogs look as if they were going to take off in my car. I know that if they could, they would have driven off and left me behind.

Kodah has always had a need to carry a toy around with him wherever he goes. For a long time his favorite was a warthog that we nicknamed "Wartie." "Wartie" was almost a security blanket for Kodah when he was younger. When he went out in public, "Wartie" went with him. I remember I had participated in a bike ride that started in Lansing and went all the way to the to the Mackinac Bridge. My little sister, Lisa, was watching over the dogs while we were gone. I had asked that she bring Kodah to Mackinac when she came to pick us up. After a very long four days, I was pedaling into the final town. In sight was the local high school, which was our finishing point. Lisa was walking Kodah on a leash through all the people, and in his mouth was his "Wartie." When I got closer to him and yelled his name, he turned and his tail began moving as fast as it could. He was making these sounds like a little lost puppy, but he never let that warthog go. Kodah continued to move about, meeting and greeting people as he walked along. He carried that toy in his mouth the entire time. Over the years he has outgrown his need to carry around a toy, but he still grabs one from time to time and puts his smiley face on and parades around for all to see. Kodah still to this day attempts to steal the onlooker's attention when we are out dogsledding. He still feels all the attention needs to be on him even without his props. Lately he likes people to hear him, though, so he can't have toys occupying his mouth.

Kodah has been that light I lost in my life when Toby died. He has been there for me through so much. He has a gift of patience and kindness that I don't find in many dogs that I encounter, including some of my other current dogs. I believe Kodah truly was meant to spend his life with me. He was saved for a reason, and I think he still has that guardian angel watching over him from above.

Sleeps
with
dogs

I Am the Chosen One (Kodah's Story)

Well, I am not trying to brag, but I have had a girl eating out of the palm of my hand since she got me. I can still recall the day that she came to get me. My life until that point had consisted of living outside with all my siblings. We had a warm doghouse to sleep in, but it was nothing compared to where she was taking me. She brought an older woman with her to come and get me. They both loved on me so much, and I gave them a ton of kisses back. It was a long ride back to where they were taking me. On the way home, I realized that I was starting to not feel good.

Once we arrived at my new home, I was feeling very sick. I could not keep my food or water down, and all I wanted to do was sleep. The next morning I was not feeling any better, but maybe worse. The young girl had to leave very early in the morning, but the older lady stayed home with me. She kept trying to feed me a nasty pink liquid. "Enough, lady, okay? I don't like it, and I don't feel good!" When I refused one thing, she would go get another thing for me to try. I was like, "Lady, are you for real?" If she was sick, she wouldn't want nasty, pink liquid or gooey, white muck, either. She called it yogurt and she said it would help me, but I think not! Who makes this stuff?

When the young girl arrived home later that day, she took me outside for, like, my thousandth trip. My poor body had enough bathroom breaks for the time being. She then took me in her car, and we drove to a place that smelled like a zoo. There were so many animal smells. A man there smelled like all the animals, too. I liked to call him the animal man from the zoo. He was talking to the girl, and then the next thing I knew, she was crying and holding on to me so tightly. When she had calmed down, they took me to a back room, where they put two pinching things into both of my front legs. Connected to these pinching things were hoses that led to bags of water that were hung over my head. All I wanted to do was sleep.

I stayed at the zoo for a number of nights, and the girl came to visit me on many occasions. It was a slow process to start to feel better and every day I tried to eat something, but it just wouldn't stay down. I felt miserable, and it didn't seem to be getting better any time soon.

One day the girl came back to see me and she was very upset. I could sense it the moment I walked into the room with her. She was sitting slumped over on the floor, and I wanted to help her. So I walked over and sat in her lap and just let her hold me. She cried and cried but I just sat there because I could sense she needed me. I didn't understand what it was that had her so upset, but I was going to be there for her like she was for me.

That night something in me changed. I started to feel better, enough that I wanted to eat something. The kind animal man brought me some soft food. I ate like I hadn't eaten in weeks. It tasted so good, and for once in a long time, it stayed down. I then tried to drink some water. It was so cold and fresh that it awakened every taste bud in my mouth. It stayed down, as well. That night I slept so well and awoke to find myself feeling even better. I ate more food and drank more water. The sickness I felt before was gone. The animal people all cheered and were so happy I was eating. I stayed one more night at the zoo, and the next day, the girl came back, but this time she took me home with her.

It took some time before I was back to feeling like myself again, but I knew I was home. The sadness the girl was feeling all the time slowly started to fade away. She took me everywhere with her. I went to stores that had treats for me (and at eye level, too), I went for long walks, I even went to Dogville, and when I was a big boy I joined the other dogs to go out running. My first time running was like nothing else I had ever experienced. The feeling of the snow crunching beneath my feet and the smells along the trail were intoxicating, and my mind was finally set free. I was running and nobody was stopping me, well, except when the girl said stop. Teeka made me stop, and you always listen to Teeka.

When I go places I want people to know that I am there. So when my girl takes me to stores that smell like animals, the moment I walk in the door I say, "Hello!' Of course I do that in the loudest voice possible, too. I like to repeat it about ten times until other people want to come pet me. I have learned that this tactic works great for getting attention. Once they come over and pet me, if they kneel on the ground, I will sit on them to ensure they do not stop petting me. It worked every time.

One of the trips that I went on took me to a farm in the middle of nowhere. I was a good boy and was allowed to be let off the leash, but this place had smells I had never experienced before and I couldn't stop following them. My girl was running after me and yelling my name, but I couldn't focus. I had to find out what was causing the smells! I ran through meadows, down hills, through mud, and then I found them. They were tall, long-legged fat things that were mean. I just wanted to get up close and smell them, but they would get defensive and chase me. I kinda thought it was fun. Then my girl came running into the picture, and I sensed she was scared. She grabbed me and pulled me up a tree. Well, as far as we could make it up the tree anyway. The four-legged beasts all gathered below the tree, but then they went away as fast as they had come. My girl grabbed my collar and ran with me back through the mud, up the hill, and through the meadow. She doused me with a hose filled with cold water, and back in the truck I went. I thought it was a grand ol' time, but I don't think she shared the same thoughts as me.

I had the girl eating out of my paw. She would let me do just about anything I wanted. I was not a fan of jumping onto things, and I liked when she helped me. I made a point to only put my two front feet on things, and then all I'd have to do was just give her that look. The look where I smiled, looked at her with deep, brown eyes, and then bellowed as loud as I could. It worked to perfection every time. I know how to work the situation to my advantage, because this girl loved me so much she would do anything for me. I had a soft spot for her, too.

My girl was gone during the night on most occasions. The older man that I grew up with came to visit us at our new house one day. He was making so much noise and chopping pieces of wood to build a house of wood for us. It was huge! We were moving into a castle. It had a pool inside, along with fans that blew cool air on us to keep us cooled down in the summer heat. Well, he left the door open to our backyard, so I snuck out undetected. I ventured through the neighboring houses, smelling the grass along the way, but then a new scent filled my nostrils. It was sweet, and there were many people gathered around this place. I scooted on over and gave the biggest "hello" I had. Everyone turned and laughed at me. I started to bat my big brown eyes, sit, shake, and lie down, and before I knew it I was being served bowls of sweet, cold cream. It was so delicious. I kept up my tricks, and the treats kept coming. I stayed there all afternoon despite the many vehicles driving around yelling my name. Like anyone in their right mind would want to leave this? My stomach was so full by the time I headed home, I was feeling a little ill but it was so worth it.

My life is great! I get to spend most of my time with my girl because I make her take me everywhere with her. Sometimes she says no and I pout, but most of the time she says yes. I don't mind just going for a ride and sitting in the car as long as I'm with her, That's all that matters.

Rhyno

I came across Rhyno in a very strange way. I thought it was one of those online ads that were too good to be true, but I decided to inquire anyway. Rhyno was a one-year-old full-bred Alaskan malamute. The owner had many dogs and realized she had to find homes for some of them. Rhyno was bred be a show dog, but he had one fault: his ears did not stand up. So I am staring at this floppy-eared giant who looks like he doesn't have a clue in the world, and I couldn't help but make an appointment to go meet him.

My mother and I drove south for a couple of hours to find a house in the middle of the country. We drove down many back roads, making turn after turn. It seemed like it took forever, but we finally made it. A long, twisting dirt road led me up to an old white farmhouse nestled among giant oak trees. As we got out, we were greeted by an Alaskan malamute, a German shepherd, and a poodle. There weren't any kennels at that point that I could see, but I could hear the dogs. I was not allowed to see the kennel area, but the sounds indicated there were numerous dogs on the property. Rhyno was mildly underweight and had no social skills when I first got him. But I fell in love and took him home with me that day.

When we arrived back home, I left Rhyno in the care of my mother because I had to go to class. He was an anxious wreck. My mother had to keep him on a leash because he would pace back and forth through the house. He could not be out with the other dogs yet because he was not socialized enough to be unsupervised. So there was my poor mother sitting in her living room holding a giant Alaskan malamute on a leash and attempting to watch TV. I am sure that it was a sight to see. I could only imagine… Just as she would get into a show, her right arm would get jerked out of its socket by Rhyno attempting to move. I still laugh over and over imagining the sight of those two. She told me that night he would literally fall asleep sitting up, and when he would begin to topple over, he would wake himself back up. Rhyno did relax over the course of a few days, and I slowly introduced him to my pack. He became familiar with his new home and new family and settled in nicely.

Rhyno does not have as many tales to tell as my other members of the pack. He has, however, grown into one of the biggest members of my pack. Rhyno is now one hundred and twenty-five pounds, compared to the seventy pounds he was when I first got him. He is seven years old now and is the biggest momma's boy out of the bunch.

Rhyno's one fault that has driven me nuts is his leash walking. If I walk him on a leash and it isn't at the pace that he prefers, he pulls, and he pulls very hard. So I have gotten one of the special anti-pull leashes, which has developed into a new trick for Rhyno, who spins in circles while walking. We call it the "Rhyno 180."

Rhyno behaves very well while dogsledding, but it is when we are going at a speed, like walking, that behavioral problems can arise. He is one of my best pulling dogs, and since he is the biggest, his position, or his job, is as a wheel dog, but he is learning to run lead, too. A wheel dog is the dog in the back closest to the sled. Since he is one of my biggest dogs, he is one of my strongest and can handle pulling the weight of the sled. Rhyno is a fun-loving dog and he sometimes has no regard for his size. He loves to be as close to you as possible. When he attempts to lie beside you, he moves extra slow, as if he knows what he is doing might be wrong but he's going do it anyway.

I decided to make a move shortly after college to Traverse City, Michigan. I moved there from the Lansing area to enjoy the opportunity of a higher snowfall during the winter season. I rented a house that was a couple of miles from Grand Traverse Bay. A long, paved trail circled the bay. The dogs and I spent many evenings walking by the bay when the heat of the summer day was subsiding. When people came across me walking my sled team, it tended to draw some attention, and Rhyno was the distinctive one that everyone wanted to pet.

One night I was walking the dogs along our local marina. Mind you, some of the boats harbored in Traverse City cost more than my house does. That night a lady came running from her very large boat and wanted to inquire about the dogs. Rhyno, of course, was her favorite. What's not to love about a dog who cocks his head from side to side when you speak as if he is trying to understand every word you are saying? She then proceeded to invite the dogs and me aboard her boat for some caviar and tea. It was a very kind offer, but visions of the events that could unfold started to spread quickly through my mind. The dogs would get loose, eat all the caviar, and then decide to eat her boat for dessert. I reluctantly and kindly declined her offer before any damage happened, and we went on our way.

Rhyno has a taste for sleeping on very plush surfaces. At my rental house in Traverse City, there were no screens in the windows, and most of them were actually painted shut. The only window I could open was the one in my bedroom. My bedroom window was also the only window that had access to the dog's kennel. Many summer nights I would leave my bedroom window open to help keep my house cool while I was away at work. And countless mornings I would come home to a surprise left by Rhyno. My bedroom was very small, and I could barely fit my bed in it. My bed edged up to the window that sided up to the dog kennel. Rhyno would take it upon himself to place his head through my window, grab a hold of my comforter, and pull it out into the dog kennel. My pillows were usually all on top of the comforter so they would go out, as well. So in the morning I would come home after a long night at work and find him, fast asleep on my comforter and pillows outside on the ground. This act would take place so many times that I just would deal with a stuffy house when I would come home each morning and keep my bedroom window shut.

We attempted to follow one of the *Dog Whisperer* techniques on many of our outings, which I did find very helpful. I purchased a backpack for each of the dogs and patches to place on them that said,

"Please don't pet me, I'm working." They always look to any passerby to pet them, offer them treats, or just out of their own curiosity they wanted to go see them. I decided to put these backpacks to good use so we would not be sidetracked as we went strolling to the dog bakery in town. I had to use these backpacks to help keep Rhyno under control when we were out walking.

I purchased what should have been a month's worth of cookies, but for my pups it would only last a week. I placed the cookies in the backpacks and we went on our way. So now the backpacks were filled to the gills, and my poor dogs were having a difficult time walking and not hitting things. This was not due to the weight but because it doubled their width and they were constantly walking into things. It was hard not to laugh at this, but I knew it was frustrating for the dogs. Rhyno had very little patience with walking, so the backpack filled with the weight of the cookies made my life so much easier. It also kept my shoulders in their sockets because he couldn't jerk me around with the leash. So lesson learned, never fill the dogs' backpacks with dog bakery treats to prevent anxiety attacks while walking.

During the winter months, we participate in many dogsled outings. Panda, my oldest, still likes to come along and run alongside the sled as long as he can. He was trained this past winter to ride on the sled. Panda is not your typical dainty Siberian husky/Alaskan malamute mix. He is a hearty ninety-pound boy. When he was first riding along, Rhyno did tend to get discouraged. Rhyno is a wheel dog along with Kodah. Once Panda got on the sled the first couple of times, Rhyno would stop, turn, and stare. Eventually he would keep running, but he was always checking back every few seconds to check if what he was seeing was for real. If he could talk, I think he might say, "Why am I carrying this lard butt?" I have many pictures that I have taken showing the look he was giving. Regardless, Panda is quite content in the sled bag and continues to ride along and enjoy himself.

In the summer months I do not use the doghouse in the back of my truck. I usually just load the dogs up for short distances to the beach and let them ride in the back. Rhyno has taken it upon himself to stand on the wheel hub in the bed of my truck and let his floppy ears fly in the wind like he is super dog. I also leave the rear window to the bed of my truck open so they can hear me if I am speaking to them. One day Rhyno thought he would attempt to fit through the window. His luck and his body size were not in his favor that day. His big body got stuck, leaving his rear end flapping in the wind on the way to the beach. The beach is only about a mile down the road from our house. To witness a very large dog's rear end hanging out must have been quite a sight. I received many looks of disbelief from people as we drove by, and when we reached the lake, he had finally managed to get himself loose. I still wonder from the passerby's perspective how strange that must have looked.

Rhyno has always been able to pay attention to the fine details around him. The television provides a great opportunity to occupy his mind when it is on, especially Animal Planet. Rhyno will approach the television when a dog is on, get as close as possible, and then attempt to pursue the dog moving across the screen. He has hit his head a couple times against the TV while attempting to get the dog on the screen, but then he realizes that as hard as he works it will not get him anywhere. It makes me laugh to see him turn his head from side to side, attempting to make sense of the situation occurring in front of him. I am always curious what he is thinking, llike, *Why are these animals right in front of me and I can't smell, touch, or catch them?*

Rhyno and Kodah have minds that act and think very similarly. One day we were cleaning out our collection of nineties sunglasses, and we thought we would try them out on my two giants. The sunglasses were the dark black, square-shaped lenses, with hot neon sides. When we had placed them on the dogs, they sat in place for a few moments trying to understand what had just happened. "Why did the room get dark?" Soon they began to walk around the house as if nothing was wrong. They posed for pictures, Kodah with his grin on and Rhyno looking like he hadn't a clue in the world what was going on. Secretly these two love to have their photos taken. They carried on for a while just walking around thinking they were the coolest dogs in the neighborhood. It was entertaining to all the guests in my house, and it soon turned into a photo shoot.

Another one of my favorite Rhyno moments took place when I had to get a rental car while my truck was being repaired. The car they gave me as a replacement for a Ford F-150 was a Fiat. A Fiat was basically the size of a clown car you would see in the circus. It had two doors, was a bright purple color, and was maybe a third of the length of my truck. I could see the dogs and I performing a circus show with that car. How many dogs can fit into a Fiat? Just like how many clowns can fit into a clown car? Luckily it was summer, and I did not need to take the dogs anywhere.

I had let the dogs out when I got home from work, and they were out running around the backyard. I then realized I had left my phone in the car, so I went back outside to grab it and I did not shut the front door of my house very tight. That was all the opportunity they needed. Rhyno and Kodah busted out.

They began rampaging through my neighborhood, and I went trailing after them in my cute little clown car. I must say, that little car can take corners on a dime. When I caught up to them at one of my neighbor's houses, I realized it was going to be tricky to fit these two in the little car. They came to me with no problem. and I loaded them into the car. Kodah took the shotgun position and Rhyno took the backseat. Now Rhyno basically consumed the entire backseat and his head was crouched into the ceiling. Thankfully, this car was equipped with a moon roof. I then opened the moon roof to relieve Rhyno's cramped quarters and we drove back. As we passed my neighbors, they were laughing hysterically. There in that compact car sat giant Kodah in the front seat and Rhyno riding along with his head peering out the moon roof the entire way back. When I reached my driveway and got out, I decided to take a look for myself at how strange we must have looked. There sat Kodah in the front passenger seat basically occupying any space he could, and Rhyno still sat in the backseat with his head looking out the moon roof. I guess if the circus was in town, they probably would have hired us.

Anyone who owns an Alaskan malamute is aware of the vocalizations that come from them. There is a distinct difference between my huskies and my malamutes. Rhyno has been scolded on more than one occasion for many different things. He always listens but thoroughly enjoys back-talking me the entire time. I imagine if I had a child, this would be equivalent to a temper tantrum. Rhyno is preparing me for motherhood in the future by breaking me in early. He will bow down and shake his head from side to side and whoo-whoo-whoo-whoo me until he feels he has put his final word in. Anyone who owns a malamute can totally relate, I am sure, to this behavior. Anytime Rhyno feels the need to put his two cents in, the response I get is always the same, whoo-whoo-whoo-whoo.

Since I got Rhyno, he has filled my life with so many memories. He has taught me lessons in life about being more responsible and that I need to put others first. When you become a pet owner, you have to devote your time to them to make sure they are well taken care of. Rhyno has required a little extra time out of my life to fulfill his needs, but it's prepared me for more dogs to come.

Why Do I Even Bother? (Rhyno's Story)

My name is Rhyno, and I'm what people call the "sad sack" of the group. My ears have always hung low, and people just assume that I am sad. It's quite the contrary, actually, because I am so happy and full of energy that I could never be sad. I came to this life through the girl. The girl came to get me at the house I was staying at. I stayed outside in my kennel with many other kennels surrounding me filled with canines. I started to develop a bit of a stir-crazy mentality sitting in there all the time until she came.

When she came and got me, she took me home to live with four other canines. They brought me inside a building, and I had never been in one before. It was filled with so many sights and sounds. She kept me on a leash because I was acting a little crazy, but it's because I was so excited I couldn't contain myself. I wanted to smell this and smell that, but she told me I had to calm down. It was just so hard. The girl had to leave, but I stayed in the house with the older lady and on the leash. I kept trying to go and explore, but she kept me on a tight leash. Tough old bird, she was. Eventually my exhaustion got the best of me. I started to fall asleep in any place I could, and sometimes that meant standing up.

I like to live life at my own pace. I am not fond of walking at slower paces. If they make me go for a walk and not a run, I make sure it is the most miserable time of their lives. I spin circles, I jump, and I yelp. It annoys them because they are always yelling, "Rhinoceros, Rhinoceros, no, no!" I laugh to myself a lot when this happens.

Sometimes my girl will shorten my leash and make me walk right beside her. I hate that because it ruins all my fun. I am forced to behave then.

One day I snuck out of the house with Kodah. It was so much fun running around the neighborhood, peeing on all the bushes I could, and just being free. I love to run and I love to run fast. My girl came after us in this little piece of metal that barely made a sound. She made Kodah and me get in the car. She was crazy! I could barely fit in that thing. Of course, Kodah, being the spoiled prince that he was, took the front seat, which made me go in the back. He always gets what he wants anyways, and the rest of us have to live with the leftovers. There was absolutely no head room in this tin can at all. I had to sit hunched over in my person's face. Thank goodness my person was thinking, and she opened up the ceiling of the tin can. I was able to sit and not hunch over so my back didn't cramp up. It was a short trip back, but people stared at me. I would have given them my autograph but she kept driving.

The girl spent many nights away from us, and we would all go to sleep in our kennel. It was cozy and was right next to the house where she lived. We were allowed inside but she wouldn't let us stay inside when she was gone. She often would leave a hole open to the house at night when she left, and right inside the hole was her bed. I loved lying on her blankets and swimming through the pillows. Sometimes I would just bring them right into my kennel. I knew I wasn't allowed to be inside, but I didn't think she would mind them coming outside. No rule breaking that way was how I saw it. She'd come home in the morning and be astonished at my creativity. Yes, I am quite proud of it myself, too.

She also trained me to run with the other canines while pulling her in tow. It was fantastic! I was never allowed to run in the front for a long time, and it could be because I had issues with running in straight lines. Nevertheless, I still loved going. I could pull longer and stronger than anyone on the team! Well, okay, not Teeka. She was one tough woman.

During the hot summer months, my person would only take me out for walks. I am guessing because it was too hot out, but I wanted to run. So I begin to protest and whine by spinning in circles and jumping on her. I have to give her credit because one day she got creative. She strapped something to my bag and it was heavy. I had to focus so hard while wearing this thing that I couldn't even think about jumping or spinning. She made me wear it on every outing we went on. Sometimes, though, it was filled with lots of goodies, and it was strapped to me. I had total control of where these treats went. It was awesome.

My life is fulfilled with love, exercise, and discipline. I love it and I wouldn't want to live anywhere else. I have my own private room for when my person is gone, unlimited treats (but I only get one at a time, darn it), and comfy couches for my choosing. I live the life of a king, and I do not feel like an Eeyore despite what everyone thinks I look like.

Malakai

Malakai is the first female that I have ever owned. I came upon Malakai at a rescue in Grand Rapids, Michigan. Her mother had been dropped off pregnant, and she was a purebred Alaskan malamute. Malakai was my third pick of the litter, and she would turn out to hold a very special place in my heart. I got her as an eight-week-old puppy. She is a malamute mix and would prove to be the most challenging dog I have ever owned. She has a thick, deep black coat with gray undertones and a beautiful well-marked mask. She has two different-colored eyes, one blue and one brown. She has a large, deep chest, a big belly, and tiny hips.

She also has the most nicknames out of my pack, such as Mal, Mali, El Diablo, and Elsie. Mal and Mali are just short for her name, but she acquired the other names due to the nature of her attitude and body weight. Malakai was a spitfire as a puppy. She seemed to think she was top dog at a very young age. She'd attempt to steal food from the other dog's bowls, take their toys when they had them, and be first at everything she did. As she grew, so did the size of her enormous attitude.

Most of the stories I have to tell are going to come from this little girl. She is a short and stout little thing, but she packs the power of an elephant. When she runs, she pulls a lot of the weight of the sled. She has become a very dominant member of my pack, and I have had to pull her in check many times. Mali still attempts things now and then, but overall her dominance has dwindled.

Malakai earned the nickname Diablo from my brother Adam. He gave this to her when she would try to pick fights with the senior and larger members of my pack, like Rhyno and Kodah. Of course, my boys would always correct her and put her back in her place. Mal has a personality that is strong and assertive among my pack, but it usually gets her into trouble. She always gets into something that constantly keeps me on my toes.

Malakai and my landscaping have never truly gotten along. She will eat and dig up whatever she is in the mood for. Trees seem to be her specialty. I once planted a beautiful Japanese maple in my newly landscaped backyard. One evening I was looking for her and I could not find her. I called and called but she wouldn't come. It was dark outside and I only have one porch light to light up my backyard. After about five minutes, I realized that she must have gotten out somehow, but then again the other dogs would have followed. So she must still be in my backyard. It was then that I saw a small body hiding behind my Japanese maple. When I looked closer, I saw Mal standing behind it with her mouth clutched to one of the tree branches. She had just been standing there frozen, thinking, *If I don't move, she will not know I am here and what I am doing.*

Her eyes were fixed on me, and she knew then I had seen her. I yelled, "Malakai," and she dropped to the ground, feet up in the air, and tail just a thumping. I couldn't help but laugh at her antics and how she thought if she didn't move I would never know what she had been up to. That tree did not stand a chance after that. Only a few days later, she had chewed through it like a beaver on a mission. I ended up replacing the tree three times, but they all met the same fate. I finally just put a cement birdbath in its place. Secretly I had my own personal win on this one: "Try to eat that, Malakai!"

One winter a snowstorm hit with thick, heavy snow and brought down many tree branches in my yard. There was a very large pine tree that had a big branch collapse down on my fence in the yard. I managed to move the limb off the fence and left it on the ground. It was about half a foot in diameter and about ten feet long with extending branches off it. I decided I would tend to it later and it could remain on the ground until then. I had left the dogs in the backyard to play, and I went inside the house. I was lying on the couch when out of my peripheral vision I could see something moving across the back lawn. My deck is high off my house and the backyard is low in comparison.

All I could see were the branches off this tree limb slowly making their way across my backyard. When I got up to assess what was going on, Malakai was at the helm. She was dragging the entire tree limb across my backyard on the way to her kennel. The entrance to the kennel was the size of your typical household door. She kept backing up and trying again and again to get the large limb into the kennel, but with the branches extending out from the limb, it was double the size of the kennel door. She put forth a grand effort, but the limb was simply not going to fit. So I had a large tree limb blocking my kennel and one very sticky, sappy dog.

Pine trees, I would soon learn, would be her favorite tree to chew on. I used to have three little pine trees in my backyard that were arranged neatly in a row by my back fence line. As of today, I have only one remaining. I have caught her many times in the act, grabbing a hold of the tops of the pine trees and just shaking them from side to side ripping off the branches. Eventually there was nothing left to the top of the tree, and so she began to eat them in half just as she did the Japanese maples. I've never figured out whether she thought she was cleaning her teeth or trimming my trees for me. It didn't seem to matter if Malakai received daily exercise, she would still find something to destroy. Maybe she could get a job with an electric company for tree clearing.

My father had helped build a small retaining wall in my backyard for me to fill with beautiful flowers. In the center of the beautiful landscaped area is where the Japanese maples had met their fate. Meanwhile, I had planted a variety of flowers such as hostas, Gerber daisies, petunias, and lots of shrubbery. I paid a lot of money to plant this arrangement, and I put a lot of time and effort into it, as well.

I left for work that night when I completed it, and when I arrived home the next morning, I was horror struck. Somehow the dogs had gotten out of their kennel and had eaten my landscaping. I don't mean they had dug it up or chewed on it: I mean, it was missing altogether in my backyard.

It wasn't difficult to narrow down who the culprit was. She had a rim of dark black soil around her muzzle, and her legs were stained red from the mulch I had just put there the day before. The fact that she kept her distance from me when I was out investigating the damage gave her away, as well. Then when I said her name, boom, she was down to the ground, legs up in the air, and ears pinned to her head, as if saying, "I am so sorry! I just needed a snack."

She gave herself away every time she did something. Malakai had consumed over four hundred dollars of landscaping plants in one night. It was tough not to be devastated. I was working two jobs, and to throw money away like that was difficult. I took my time to replace what she had done and eventually installed small fencing around the retaining wall to protect the plants. It seemed to work like a charm.

Malakai has redecorated my house in many ways over the years. She developed a taste for the color pink for a while. I had a pink highlighter on my computer desk and she found it. At the time I worked midnights. When I came home I soon discovered that Malakai had painted herself a pretty pair of hot pink leg warmers. It took me a while to understand what she had gotten into. I searched all over my house, and in my spare bedroom I found the results. She had chewed apart a pink highlighter and had added beautiful pink accents to my lovely light green carpet. I managed to get most of the color out, but it was easy to spot on the carpet which area she had decided to create her masterpiece on. It was not but a few weeks later that she found another pink highlighter. Why she would find the pink ones I do not know: pink is my least favorite color and there are many other colors to choose from.

I woke up one morning and again, she was marked on both front legs with pink highlighter. The search began to see where she had committed this act, and I found it on a section of my couch. I have a beautiful cream-colored suede couch that must have been just a little too boring for her and she decided to add a little pink. Getting pink highlighter out of a cream-colored suede couch is not easy. I recommend scotch guarding all of your couches if you are going to own dogs. I still have the couch and the evidence is fading, but the memory still remains.

Mal has always been in love with water. She can come across a source of water no matter the size and she will play in it. So you can only imagine how excited she gets when she comes across a body of water that she can swim in.

When I used to live close to Traverse City, we would go swimming in the bay often. One day we went out around dusk. It was very close to the Cherry Festival in Traverse City, Michigan, and the number of people coming to the city was growing. The boats were lining the bay where I let the dogs go in. Most of the boats were anchored, and nobody was on them except one pontoon boat that was having a lot of fun. Mal was swimming around the water with Kodah, Rhyno, and Panda. Then she caught a glimpse of the pontoon boat and could hear the people aboard. She began to swim out into the bay toward them. Mali was like Nessie the sea monster, swimming effortlessly and fluently in the water. She reached the boat, and the people on board caught a glimpse of her and decided to help her get on board with them.

So, there was my chubby little girl getting pulled out of the bay with water rushing off her like a waterfall and onto their incredibly nice boat. She then, of course, shook off and dowsed all the people within standing distance of her. I could hear their screams from the shore. I could see her on the boat from the shore, and she greeted everyone with a wet, wagging body.

She was moving quickly over to each person like she was saying, "Hi, hi everyone, I'm Malakai!"

I called for her to come back, but she would not get off the boat. Luckily one of my friends happened to pass by, and I asked them to please hold on to my other "good" dogs on the shore. So there I went. I kicked off my shoes and went swimming in my clothes after Malakai. I wasn't planning on going swimming that evening, but Malakai had other plans for me. When I reached the boat, she then realized who I was and came to me. I'm sure if dogs could talk, she would be saying, "Hey, Mom, look at all these fun people. They have lots of good-smelling food, Mom!" She required a little assistance getting off the boat, but soon Mal and I were swimming our way back to shore. My other dogs waited eagerly, and my friend was laughing so hard at what she had just witnessed. Unfortunately, this would not be Malakai's only encounter with a boat in the middle of a lake.

I took Kodah and Mal with me to a local lake in the middle of summer to cool off. They are my most water-loving dogs, so that is why they accompanied me. It's a no-wake lake and many fishermen come there to avoid the noise and crowds of the bigger lakes. While they were swimming around, a small fishing boat was making its way across the lake in front of us. It caught the attention of both of my pups, and they proceeded to swim after it. If they weren't running away from me, they were swimming away from me.

They did end up catching the small fishing boat that was oar-operated, but due to the boat's size and shape they could not get on board. The fishermen attached rope to their collars and brought them back to shore to me. So there was this boat making its way back, and Kodah and Mal were swimming on each side of it. Since the boat was oar-powered, it helped with keeping pace for my dogs. Once they reached the shore, the fisherman said that they had never caught two Siberian huskies while fishing before and this was one for the books. I tried to find humor in it, but I was fuming and could feel my blood pressure rising. I thanked them ever so much and decided Kodah and Mal needed to do one more mile loop for that stunt.

My dogs have a routine that falls alongside of mine. They know that when I come home in the morning, they are to do their business, then it's inside and to bed. The only time my dogs get treats is when I go to bed.

They also know that when I wake up, it's their dinnertime. Keep in mind I work the night shift, so my schedule is opposite from everyone else's. Malakai has decided to now hang out with me in the bathroom and be a bossy little girl while I try to get ready for work. She will poke her head into the shower multiple times and bark, then run away fast. Then she will creep back, knock my shampoo and conditioner in on me, and run away.

While I am brushing my teeth, blow-drying my hair, or getting dressed, she will bark at me and then move just out of distance for me to reach her, wagging her tail, bowing her head, and sticking her butt up in the air. I still am trying to figure out what it is she is doing. Attention, attention, attention. That is all she wants. So I cannot possibly ever get ready for work without Mal barking and sassing me while I am getting ready. I now have to add an extra fifteen minutes to get ready for the number of times I have to pause in my routine to stop and deal with Malakai. She is truly a unique dog.

Malakai has a special ability to open a sliding door when it is shut. She has on many occasions opened my sliding door to the backyard and allowed my entire pack in my house. One morning I came home from work, and my large picture window was covered in dirt. I was trying to rationalize in my mind how this could have happened. "Do I have a ghost?" "Are there intruders in my house who are camouflaging my window?" When I entered the house, I was shocked at what I saw. On my floor and couch were the remains of my compost bin from the backyard. Malakai had opened the slider door, broken in to my compost bin, and had been bringing treasures in all night long while I was at work. I had remains of bananas, squash, and potatoes all over my house! She also thought that I needed my garbage emptied in the bathroom and that should clutter the floor, as well. I was furious with what I saw. The sad part was, she knew what she had done was wrong and the Malakai flop happened…again. She dropped to floor like she always does when she is in trouble, with all four feet up in the air, ears pinned back, and squinting eyes.

After surveying the rest of the damage, I realized the plate of brownies my sister had made and had left on the counter was missing, as well. The plate remained but its contents could not be found. Malakai has an ability to always eat things she should not, and the brownies fell victim to El Diablo. She, of course, was fine. I know that I could blame the other dogs because they were all with her, but deep down I knew who the ringleader was. The amount of things her body can digest and tolerate could only be explained as a miracle.

Malakai has always been one to mess around in my kitchen and steal things from the counter. It was winter, and I had just made a big pot of chili. I love my chili spicy so it was loaded with hot sauce and jalapeños. I removed it from the stove to cool while I got ready to go to work. Once I was done getting ready, I realized Malakai had not come in to the bathroom to bother me like usual. When I called her she came, and to my surprise a rim of red covered her muzzle. I knew instantly she had gotten into my chili. When I went downstairs, I realized she didn't only get into my chili, but she consumed the entire pot! Her stomach was going to be very unhappy with her in a matter of hours. When I left for work, I placed her in the outside kennel because repercussions were soon to follow.

When I arrived home the next morning and let her out, she moved like lightning to go to the bathroom. Through the rest of the day, poor Malakai would go in and out every hour. I ended up having to apply Desitin to her rear end after each time out to the bathroom. The poor baby was getting a very sore bum. The things I do for my dogs are unbelievable. You can bet your last dollar she also did not tolerate me applying diaper rash cream. If you can picture wrangling a crocodile and a kangaroo at the same time, I imagine we would have looked pretty close to that. I now leave the chili on the rear portion of the stove to cool and not the front.

For anyone who owns a husky, you know how time-consuming it is to keep their coats in shape. Professional grooming was too expensive for seven dogs, so I bought a professional blow-dryer, shampoos and conditioner, and many supplies. Most of my dogs have grown to love bathing and the blow-dryer, but not young Malakai. Of course, this is done outside of my house and in the backyard. My other dogs are lined up waiting their turns, but she is at the farthest point of my backyard that she can get from me. When it comes time for her to get wet, I have to place a leash around her and drag her over to the tub and dryer. The sounds coming out of her when the bathing begins could wake the entire neighborhood. It sounds like a chainsaw mixed with animal caught in a trap, high-pitched wailing that is mixed with a few barks, and then gargling sounds as she chokes the last breath out of herself on the leash.

She will carry on through the entire bath, making herself hoarse as we near the end. Once the bathing portion has been completed, it is time for the blow-dryer. She has to remain on the leash because she will try to escape. This is where the flopping begins to take place. She looks like Free Willy and Flipper and the same time, rearing up on her rear legs, tossing her legs in the air, and then continuing this bucking nonsense the whole time. It has its benefits as I get a great shot at drying her abdomen and chest. She has been getting this done a year or so now, and she still continues with these crazy antics.

One fall Malakai began to act not her usual self. She became very lethargic and not wanting to eat. I continued to monitor her throughout the day and she only began to get worse. When she would attempt to relieve herself, she would yelp in extreme pain and run around as if she had been stung by something. Concerned with what I was seeing, I decided to take her in to the emergency vet. Remembering back to the previous few days, I recall it was around the time she had just devoured one of the Japanese maples. I was thinking she must have not been able to tolerate a portion of the tree that she had eaten and it had become a blockage or worse, it had perforated. When we arrived, we were placed into an examination room. There the vet went over the past days' occurrences and began to assess her. He then informed me that he would have to perform a rectal exam.

I thought, *Oh boy, she is going to give him a run for his money.* He then proceeded to take her back to another room where an assistant would be able to help. I could hear her screaming and yelping coming from all the way down the hall and through a closed door. When the vet returned her to me, he informed me, sarcastically, that she was a "delicate little butterfly."

I had to chuckle to myself because I can only imagine how difficult that must have been for the staff. He did not find any indication of a tear or a piece of material that would be causing her this pain. Abdominal X-rays were done, and yet there was nothing to see that could be the source of her pain. He had me give her some Imodium to assist in digestion and continue to monitor her.

I took her home late that evening and slept beside her on the couch. When we woke the next morning, I let her out to relieve herself again and she did it again. A loud yelp and then this time she dropped to the ground and did not move. She, of course, was all right, but just performing a little drama queen action. It was then I realized that she had not urinated since the night before, and maybe this was more urinary tract–related than gastrointestinal. I proceeded to call my vet and I was told to come right in. When we arrived, they took us in to the exam room and I gave them my story of the events that had taken place. Since she was not able to go to the bathroom, they were going to have to collect a sample themselves.

Malakai was once again taken back to an exam room and a sterile urine sample was to be obtained. The exam door was left open and once again I could hear the yelps and screams very clearly all over again. The next thing I knew, here came Malakai running down the hall, leash dragging behind her and the vet tech chasing her down. She made it back to the exam room where I was waiting and leapt into my lap as if I was going to save her. The young woman made the comment that she was a special little girl and stronger than they had expected. She'd managed to escape three vet technicians. Luckily the sample was obtained and the results were in. Malakai had a very bad urinary tract infection. It was treated with antibiotics and then a repeat urine sample would need to be obtained, but luckily I was able to avoid the catheter again. She finished her course of medication, and the second urine test proved to be negative. She was in the clear.

Shampoo and Porcupines

have two gates that enter the back of my yard. One is a very large gate with double swinging doors. The second is a small door gate that only can be opened from the inside of the yard. I was getting ready for work and the dogs were outside. My doorbell rang, but I ignored it because my head was full of shampoo. When it continued to ring, I proceeded to exit the shower, put on a towel, and answer the door. It was my neighbor informing me that all four of my dogs had gotten out. When I looked, sure enough, they were all meandering near the house across the street.

I ran out the door wearing just my purple bath towel with shampoo still in my hair. As I approached them, I told them to go back inside the house, and thankfully they did. I placed them back in the house and then went to the backyard to see how they had gotten out. I had forgotten for a brief second how my clever little Malakai was capable of opening the slider door that leads to the backyard. While I had checked the larger gate and was making my way to the other side of the fence, the slider door opened up and out piled four dogs. They headed beeline for the other gate, and sure enough it was wide open and they escaped for a second time. So, still in my towel, I raced inside, grabbed my car keys, and headed after them. I lived just a few blocks away from a very popular ice cream and coffeehouse. I caught up to them at that point, adjacent to the restaurant parking lot, and opened my tailgate to have them climb inside. Of course, Rhyno is my only capable dog to be able to jump independently into the back of the truck. So, I am holding on for dear life to the towel I have still on, and then I have to assist Malakai, Kodah, and Panda into the truck. Malakai cannot get in because she is so short, Kodah is just plain lazy, and Panda has gotten older and his vertical jump strength just isn't there anymore.

So, all the customers in the coffee shop were watching and laughing at the sight of this poor girl with shampoo in her hair, desperately holding on to her bath towel to not give them all a peep show, and loading her runaway dogs up into her truck. We continued back home, I locked the back gate and then let them all in the house. I then finished getting ready, put them all in their kennel, and headed in to work. I wish I could say that was the only time that has happened.

One morning while I was finishing up with my shift at the hospital, I got a phone call from my neighbor at work. She told me the dogs were hurt pretty badly and had gotten into a porcupine. They had somehow gotten out of my backyard and had been sitting in her front lawn all morning. When she finally got closer to them, she realized what had happened. I had fifteen minutes left in my shift, so I finished my work quickly and raced out the door. It seemed to take hours to drive home, and when I reached home I was mortified with what I saw. Panda and Kodah had so many quills in their mouths that they were unable to close them. Rhyno was the next worse and had about half the amount as the other two. Malakai had a few in her muzzle that I was able to remove. I had to contact the emergency house call vet to come because the vet offices were not open this early in the morning. My friend had also arrived at that time to see if he could be of any help—thank goodness he did.

It was not long after I made the call to the vet that he arrived at my house. When he came in and made assessments, he began to give medications to Rhyno, Kodah, and Panda to get them sedated so we could begin to remove the quills. Panda was the worst off, and we were to start with him first. Panda was placed on the island in my kitchen and was sedated. Hemostats were the only option I had to remove the barbed quills that had made their way inside his mouth, down his throat, and had covered his entire muzzle. It took around an hour and a half to remove the quills from Panda alone. When he was done, he was laid on the floor to wake up from the sedation.

Kodah was next, and he, as well, had quills surrounding his muzzle, inside his mouth, and down his throat. It was a lot of work to remove all the quills from Kodah. Another hour and a half passed by to remove them, and the same care was provided to him as Panda when he was done. I then had two sleeping giants on my floor waiting to awaken from sedation. Rhyno was the last to be cleaned up, and it also took a little more medication to get him to go to sleep due to his size. After around four hours, the vet had completed his work, I was broke, and the dogs were on the mend.

The porcupine was found in the backyard by the vet, and he had never seen one with all of the quills missing before. That porcupine had unloaded all the quills into my dogs, and unfortunately for it, it did not survive the incident. To this day we do pass by porcupines while out dogsledding, and the dogs still have the urge to go after them. Apparently learning from past experiences does not apply in the dog world.

Birdseed

Malakai has a taste for things that dogs should not be eating. Among her favorites are cupcakes, brownies, coffee, cardboard, Skittles, markers, and birdseed. I love to have a bird feeder and watch the birds come and go. I had one in the front yard of my house, but I had an extra shepherd's hook and decided to place a second one in my backyard. I bought an adorable bird feeder in the shape of a lantern. Being a new home owner, small things like this were fun.

The bird feeder was placed beside my deck among the area of my new landscaping. As time went by, I was beginning to notice sprouting sunflowers all over my backyard. I was assuming it was related to squirrels or chipmunks. But one day while I was looking out my kitchen window I spotted her. The feeder came level with one of my top decks, and she was stretching her little neck as far as it could go to lap up the sunflower seeds with her tongue. Malakai again was my culprit. Now that the birds were petrified to come to the feeder, my backyard was growing into a field of sunflowers. It was then I decided it was time to move the bird feeder back to the front yard and out of Malakai's reach. Much to my amazement, the assortment of sunflowers growing came to a halt and I wasn't refilling bird feeders every other day.

Malakai, by far out of all of my dogs, is the most comical. All of my dogs have their own distinct personalities and behaviors, but Malakai's tends to stand out the most. Not a day goes by when there is not something she does that doesn't bring a smile to my face. I love her with all my heart and know that there is a reason the first two puppies I had wanted from her litter were already chosen. I was supposed to have Malakai.

Master of Disguise (Malakai's Story)

I am the ruler of the house, the head honcho, the big cheese, or the alpha female if you really need to know. Well, okay, I try almost every second of the day to carry that title, but my person is alpha and she stops me every time I try. Sometimes all I do is look with my eyes and she knows. I want to please her with all my heart, so I listen when she tells me to stop most of the time. How have I come to live with this household of canines? I was introduced when I was just a little puppy to Panda, Kodah, and Rhyno. I was sure to let them know I was the new sheriff in town and they had better follow suit.

I may have been the small squirt of the bunch, but I was growing into a fierce, confident leader. Sure, I challenged the boys on many occasions to have them show me respect, but I learned quickly from them that was not my place. I want to do what I want to do, and when I want to do it. That is how I try to live my life. My person loves to remind me often that I need to take a time-out. She always is telling me, "No grumbles, no grumbles!" Really? That is how I express my feelings. Yeah, I may include a little lip curl now and then, and then she is like, "Ahh, Mali, Mal, no, no, no! What are you doing, no!" Okay, lady, I get it, no means no.

There are times when I just feel she has this landscaping thing all wrong. Certain plants look good and others don't. She needs to trust me when I say flowery and pine needle–like trees do not belong in landscaping. You would think she would have thanked me for removing all those dreadful-looking trees and plants. She obviously didn't get the hint when I was stealing the plants before she spent all that time digging holes and sticking them in the ground. She left us one evening to go and do what she does, so I thought I would surprise her when she came home in the morning to redesigned landscaping. I snuck out of the enclosed area she kept us in and went to work. It was while I was digging them up that I realized how tasty they actually were. The girl is always willing to fill her belly so I had a few midnight snacks. When she came home and went in the backyard, I was waiting hidden in the shadows to jump out and yell surprise, but her reaction made me think I'd better just stay put. She seemed actually livid, and I could sense her energy level was emitting anger. She instantly yelled, "Malakai!" Why would she instantly blame me? Well, she saw me and I did what I know to do best: drop to my side, pin my ears back, and tuck my tail. Don't make eye contact; don't make eye contact. I was busted because I didn't remove the dark black stains from my muzzle or feet. It also could have been that I was the only one outside the kennel. That must have been it!

I've had a little spicy side in me. You know I never met my dad, and for all I know he could have been a Chihuahua. Spicy foods are my absolute favorite, and I can't get enough of them. If I smell them, I want them and wait till someone is not looking and then it's mine. Well, she had to go get into this rain tub, which was far away from the pot of spicy goodness she just made. So I just figured I'd take a taste and see how good she had done. It was delicious and had a little kick at the end. I just couldn't help myself. I ate the entire pot. I tried to hide myself after I had consumed it, but she saw me and ran frantically over to me. She kept saying, "Let me see, let me see. Oh, Mal, what happened?" It was when she got a wet rag out that I knew I was busted. She would no longer think that I was injured and then I would get into trouble again. Yup, here it comes, "MALAKAI!" She ran to the kitchen and surveyed my damage. I tried to tell her it was great and she was a great cook, but all my efforts didn't seem to matter at that point. I might as well have been wearing the cone of shame.

It was the following morning that I realized the error in my decision from the night before. The amount of bathroom trips I made that day had to have set a world record. It was horrible. I was in pain with my stomach rumbling, passing gas all the time, and the pure, liquid fire that came out of me was enough kill a skunk. She must have felt pity for me because the next thing I knew she was slathering this paste all over my rear end. I was mortified and fought like a banshee to get away, but then all of a sudden there was instant pain relief. The goop was magic! I love her so much.

I can recall once when she left the four of us at home, we encountered the most ferocious beast ever. I wrestled with it, chased it, and watched a lot of the incident. The boys had it covered. They were protecting their queen, so I didn't have to get my nails dirty, but when it was over we were all in so much pain. We all had these sharp sticks stuck in our faces, ears, tongues, and cheeks. It wasn't long until she was home, and with her came a man who smelled like a thousand different animals. He gave the boys sticks in their legs and they went to sleep pretty quickly. She just pulled the stick out of my face with her hands. I had so many stuck in my face, I was a warrior. Well, it was more like three or four sticks in my face, but they did make me bleed…a little. The boys had thousands of sticks stuck to them, and they were asleep all day. We all recovered from this ordeal, and we vowed never to take on the small animal with sticks that shot out of his butt again.

One night I wasn't feeling the best, and I just wanted to sleep. The girl let us outside to do our business before heading to bed, and when I attempted to relieve myself, I experienced an intense burn that dropped me to the ground. She then loaded me up in the car, and I could sense she was frantic as she drove me to the place that smelled like a zoo. I hated that place. Nothing ever good came from going to that place. They took me back with her to a room. I was violated with a tiny sliver metal thing and then the animal man came in. She was talking to him for a long time, and the next thing I knew, they were leading me away from her. I was kicking and screaming to get away from them, but it was no good. That forced me to bring out the big guns, my teeth. Well, that didn't stop them because the next thing I knew I was wearing a mask that was hiding my teeth. Then the animal man did something he should have never done. I was given what I might call an inappropriate exam, but he had to search my rear end for something I already knew he would not find. How mortifying was that? I dragged him back as fast as I could to her. I climbed as best as I could into her arms and she spoke with the animal man for a while. We were soon on our way home, and I was not feeling any better.

The following morning I awoke and actually felt worse. I was groggy and in pain but I needed to pee so badly. I tried and tried but nothing happened. I'd fall over in so much pain and just lie there. What was I going to do? She then came and got me, loaded me up again in the rumbling, metal machine, and we went to another animal zoo. When we arrived there, it was a lady animal person this time. She, as well, took me away from my person. I fought with everything I had, and this time I was violated another way. What was wrong with these people? I escaped all three of their grasps by twisting like a crocodile (my person watches a lot of Animal Planet). I was free and hauled like a bat out of hell back to my person. I climbed into her lap and begged her to let me go again. The animal lady came back in the room and spoke for a while. We left shortly after, and when I got home I was rewarded with a spoonful of peanut butter. A few hours later, I was able to relive myself and the pain was improving. For days to come I received a spoonful of peanut butter twice a day and it got easier and easier to pee. I was cured!

I enjoy the sport of swimming very much. Swimming in deep water and in circles is my favorite because then I can try to catch the waves of water that my body creates. Often when I am out swimming, there are these floating houses with people on them. I like to take it upon myself to go and investigate who is on these boats and see if they would be willing to give me a snack or a nice beverage. There have been a couple of occasions that these people on the boat only took me back to shore where my person was waiting. If I had wanted to go there, I would have just swum there myself. One of them had the audacity to hang on to my collar and make Kodah and I swim their floating house back to shore. I know these things have loud, water-spraying things on the back of them that make them move fast in the water. Come on, people, that was why I swam out there in the first place.

There are these trees that grow all over where I live. They have a minty smell and taste to them when you bite into them. I love to taste a branch here and there. It is a great way to cleanse the teeth, if you know what I mean. Sure, my person tries to scrub my teeth with this nasty goop and I am sure to make it as difficult as I possibly can. When she is done attempting to accomplish something, I go and grab a piece of my tree and do some cleaning of my own. Sometimes I do get carried away, but these shrubs are so small, she will never even notice that they are missing.

Humans create the strangest things sometimes, but I have learned how to adapt to them to my advantage. They have these doors that are see-through, like they want the outside indoors but not really. It slides back and forth. Well, when she left to go places, I would take it upon myself to open that door and let myself in and out. There was nothing stopping me when she was gone. I let all my canine family out, too, and we had a party when she was gone. Her place was so clean and tidy all the time. She was constantly sweeping up my hair, brushing it off things inside, and brushing me. It can get out of control sometimes, the degree she will take things. When I let the clear door open, I was sure to bring some color from outside in. My canine family and I love to chase each other and tear up the fabric that was on the floor, to bring some mud inside to spruce the place up a bit. When she would come home in the morning, the look on her face was of total surprise. I knew she would like it; I knew she would like it. But then I sense something is off. She is not happy; she is angry. Oops, sorry, I got to run, and out the clear door I went.

One of these days the girl is going to get it. I am the ruler of this doghouse (well, only when she is gone), but it is my job to keep a confident and strong attitude. This helps keep the canines that I live with in line. I am going to eat, chew, and swim wherever I feel like going. If someone has something and I want it, I will get it. On the outside I project the image that I am the queen of the pack, but really on the inside I want nothing more than to make my person happy. I love her very much, and I can't stop my body from wiggling uncontrollably when she comes around. My life is amazing, and I am grateful that I am with her every day.

Bandit

andit is a sweet, fun-loving, adorable little boy. Now, when I say little, I mean he is a normal-sized Siberian husky, but I had been living with my four giants for so long, he seemed small. Bandit is a beautiful black-and-white Siberian husky with piercing blue eyes. I got him when he was around a year and a half old from a coworker of mine. They had a very busy lifestyle, and there was not much time for Bandit with their schedules. They had heard of me with all my dogs and wondered if I would be interested in taking him. I was unsure at first. I already had my hands full with four dogs, but Panda would be retiring soon and I would need a replacement.

When I went to their house to meet him, I did not know I would be falling in love at first sight. I arrived at their home in this beautiful country setting. Waiting inside their home while they went to get him, the anticipation built. When he entered, this gentle, blue-eyed little boy came slowly toward me and began to lick my hands. He was such a gentle and well-mannered dog that it was so hard to not want to take him home right there.

I had to work the next three nights so I did not have time to orient him properly to my other dogs. Bandit remained with the original owners while I finished out my workweek, then I went and got him. Bandit came home to live with me in the winter months at the prime of our dogsledding season. When we arrived home, my other pups were outside in the kennel. Bandit took himself on a tour of my house, checking out the other dogs' beds, toys, and food bowls. I then left him inside and went to let the others out of the kennel in the backyard.

It was a game of ring around the rosy; Bandit was placed in the garage so he could not be overwhelmed by the other dogs coming into my house. I then moved him to the backyard so he could explore at his own pace without the others smelling him.

He did his fair time of searching and smelling, and I decided to let one of my dogs come out to meet him. Kodah, since he is my gentlest and the most easygoing, met him first. Bandit froze when Kodah stepped out. Kodah eagerly went to greet Bandit and towered over poor little Bandit due to his size. (I am sure this was intimidating.) Soon Bandit relaxed and the two entered into a game of chase. Bandit went exploding through the yard with Kodah trailing pretty far. It was then I discovered the speed of a Siberian husky compared to that of a giant Alaskan malamute. Once I was confident in Bandit's behavior, I allowed one more dog at a time in to meet him until everyone was in the backyard. Before long they were tearing through the backyard with Bandit always in the lead, having the time of his life.

Bandit would prove to be the gentlest of all of my dogs. He is calm, quiet, and well behaved, except when he is around alcohol. It didn't take long for me to realize that one of his favorite beverages to drink was alcohol. It didn't seem to matter if it was beer or wine, he would beg to have some. I do not allow my dogs to have any form of alcohol whatsoever, so Bandit would have to be very sneaky about his methods. One of the employees that my mother works with was at our cabin, and he made the mistake of placing his beer mug on the coffee table. Bandit was at it so fast, he had half the glass gone before we knew what was going on. Some dogs beg for food, but not Bandit. Bandit only begs when someone is drinking beer or wine. So when friends and family come over, I have to warn them to please not leave your alcoholic beverages unsupervised if Bandit is around.

Bandit seems to be one of the popular favorites out of my group. One of his admirers is my sister-in-law, Amber. Bandit cozied up to her the first time they met, and she, too, shared the adoration for him. Time and time again I would find those two sitting secretly off to the side and she would be giving him little nibbles of whatever she had on her plate. Normally Bandit could care less about food, but he knew when Amber was around, he would get special treats. It was like keeping my eye on two little children. Bandit soon learned to follow Amber wherever she would go because he knew it was going to be his one and only chance to have forbidden food. Even still, when he would accept food from her, he was so gentle and slow.

I have not had much luck with the garage doors on my house. When I purchased my house, I had a beautiful white garage door on it. I had to always start my dogs out in the garage when we would go sledding, and then use a remote to open the door when we were ready to head out. It was late fall and I had to use the summer rig because snow had not fallen yet. The summer rig, like I said before, weighs ninety pounds and is four feet by four feet.

The floor in the garage was wet this particular day due to some rain early in the morning. When the dogs were harnessed and the door began to rise up, they bolted with a speed they had never had before. They went so fast that it clipped my garage door sensor and began to send the door back down. The dogs had by now made it under the door but the cart and I still were in the garage. Panic had set in on me and the commands fell blank to my mouth. I jumped off and they sent the cart barreling into the garage door. What happened next would best be described as the scene of a tornado. The garage door just peeled off my house like it was a tuna can. Along with the door came the garage door opener as well sending sparks flying through the garage. I stood horrified at what had just happened to my house. The cart became lodged in the door, not allowing my dogs to run free. I collected the dogs, placed them back inside, and began to think about what I was going to do.

I contacted my friend, who happened to be a handyman and we were able to locate a used garage door that he could replace my other mangled mess with. I purchased a new garage door opener and fixed everything as good as new. Who would have thought a month later, I would take out the door again with my truck. My father always said that if I didn't have bad luck, I'd have no luck at all.

I started to brainstorm at how I could possibly anchor the summer cart to prevent the dogs from pulling away with it. The problem was I would harness and attach dogs one at a time to lines. By the time I had four dogs hooked up—that was enough power to start to move my summer cart. I needed to have my garage door open when we would start our run to prevent losing a third garage door. To anchor the cart, I placed it behind my riding lawn mower, a doghouse, and a cast iron tub. While I began hooking the dogs up, of course the items began to move little by little. When the last dog was finally harnessed up, that was when everything gave way. So out of my garage went my team of huskies, my lawn mower moving in reverse, my doghouse, and my cast-iron tub with me running behind it all. I can only imagine what my neighbors must have thought.

After the garage door experience, I began to anchor them to my Ford F-150. I purchased that quick release snap which allowed me to tie them to the tow bars of my truck and, with the press of a button, release us. Now, when my dogs are getting harnessed up and preparing to go, the level of excitement can be heard all throughout the neighborhood.

One morning at my parent's cabin we were getting ready to head out for a run, but my truck was blocked in with my mother's Jeep Wrangler. I thought that would be an acceptable vehicle to use to anchor the dogs. I brought the dogs out, two at a time, hooking up the wheel dogs first. Bandit and Malakai would be my two lead dogs with Kodah and Rhyno in the back. When Mal and Bandit were hooked up, I noticed that the Jeep was beginning to move. The Jeep was not on and had been placed in park. Sure enough, those four little dogs were strong enough to pull the Jeep. It was not a drastic distance that they pulled it, but enough to move it from its original position down the driveway.

Bandit has developed into one of my best lead dogs. He listens well, and he has the speed and endurance to maintain the team over long distances. He is also my most excited dog when the harnessing begins. He will prance, spin in circles, jump in the air, and then when he is called for his turn to put his harness on, he come immediately to my feet and sit. He will sit very still, almost motionless, and allow me to harness him. He was never told or taught he had to sit to have his harness put on, which just goes to show you how gentle-natured this little boy can be. Once he is harnessed, the wild man returns full-force.

I am so thankful to have Bandit. He is such a sweet boy, and he desires any attention he can get from anyone he meets. Over the years that I've owned him, he has developed into a couch potato and dog-treat-eating machine. Bandit now needs to have his diet strictly monitored and measured or that little boy can pack on the pounds. Bandit is so sweet and wonderful, and I thank the Lord that he has become a member of my amazing pack.

Don't Bother Me, I'm Sleeping
(Bandit's Story)

When I came to this new home, I was well into my adult years of life. But I had spirit like a wildfire that couldn't be tamed. I wanted to run to my heart's content and chase the other dogs around the yard. My new people took me out to run with the other canines and we would fly like a flock of birds in the sky. We were untouchable when we were out running.

I had such a drive and passion for running for about a week. While living at my new house, I was introduced to something called a couch. The life of a couch potato was my new-found goal. Have any of you ever sat on a couch before? They are amazing! There is enough room to sprawl out, lie upside down, roll over, or even bury some bones in them, too. Couches are my new-found love, maybe even more than cookies.

Humans have this liquid that they drink that has a sour smell to it, but it is so delightful to drink. It has a bitter taste at first, but then it goes down smooth. Humans have this tendency to leave things sitting around at low heights. This makes it great for me because I am the vertically challenged one in my family. I also have no competition for this particular beverage—well, Malakai sometimes tries to push my buttons, but she is really just full of hot air. The darker the color of the liquid, the better it tastes. Oh, it is so delightful when I can get a taste of it. I have learned to have stealth techniques to sneak up and snag these containers of delectable liquids. The humans never see me coming…most of the time.

The girl in the new home that I moved into takes us canines out often to run. We even get to run when there is no snow on the ground. She takes us out on a cart with wheels. It is just this tiny little thing, and the rest of us canines can toss it around like it's nothing. She clearly did not perform her research before taking us out. One day the other canines and I were just beside ourselves to go running because the air was chilled that day, and that is our best running conditions. She hooked us up one at a time inside this area with a large door that opened from the bottom up. We just couldn't stand it. We wanted to run. The minute that door started going up, we took off like our butts were on fire. The next thing I knew, we were stopped abruptly by a loud sound. Then there she came. Oh boy, was she mad. That door was moving just too slowly. It was clearly the door's fault for not getting out of our way. She had to unhook us all, and we could not go running that day. When it was my turn to turn around and go back inside with her, I was appalled at what that door had done. It literally tried to jump off the house and follow us on our run. What a silly door!

So this place I live at has us go running on almost a daily basis, which I think is absurd. Well, let me tell you that I have now specific requirements before I will go. One, I do not run on anything but snow. Two, the temperature has to be to my liking. Three, if I am sleeping on my couch, don't even bother waking me. I don't want to go. Four, I don't want to run next to my sister Malakai. Five, do not ever make me ride in the sled. Six, if I seem excited I am just faking it. Finally, I run twenty feet and I am done. I am a sprinter, not a long-distance runner.

I have loved my life living with the canine crazy lady. She has welcomed so many new activities, people, and tastes to my life that I would never want to live anywhere else. I have had the opportunity to take many trips to lands filled with water and go running through forests filled with fresh snow. The amount of dogs that I have been able to meet and share my stories with allows my life to be fulfilled with purpose. I couldn't imagine living anywhere else or sleeping on any other surface than my couch.

Luna

Luna is a beautiful all-white Siberian husky who worked herself into my life. I had my hands full with my five, and to think of adding a sixth dog seemed unimaginable at that time. My friend downstate had contacted me to tell me that there was a husky in urgent need of a home or she was going to be euthanized through no fault of her own.

My parents only had Rocky and Teeka at that time, and I asked if they wouldn't mind taking her while I worked on finding her a home. They agreed and since the rescue was so close, they drove and picked her up. Luna had a beautiful all-white coat and bright blue eyes. This was to be her third home at the young age of one. She was very underweight when she arrived, and like many of my other dogs, she had no social skills among canines.

Luna was introduced to Rocky and Teeka, and at their old age, they did not seem to give her much thought. After a week of being at my parents' house, Luna proved that their very large fencing system was not going to contain this spirited girl. Luna would simply climb their five-foot-high chain-link fence like it was merely a game. This happened numerous times until they kenneled her in the barn during the day when they were at work to prevent an escape. This, they soon also learned, did not stop her escape antics. Inside the barn was the chain-link fence that Toby had finagled himself out of. It was ten feet high and led to the inside portion of the dog kennel. Luna simply climbed this fence, too, went through the dog door, and then climbed the outside fence before taking off. So this is how Luna came to live with me.

This dog had lacked exercise her entire life. She needed to be where she could expel this excess energy and calm those traits of the husky. I have a large fenced-in yard with a privacy fence. There would be no way for her to be able to grab a hold of the wooden panels and climb out. When Luna had arrived, she was wearing a harness. My mother said that slipping collars while on leashes was also one of her new developing tricks. Once again the other dogs were removed from the backyard, and she was allowed to sniff around and become acquainted with her new surroundings. She did attempt many times to climb my fence, but she was not able to. Luna had found her new home. I introduced her to the rest of my dogs, one at a time, until I had a pack of six huskies enjoying themselves all over my yard. Bandit would prove to be Luna's main interest. I don't know if it was because they are the same size, but they were drawn to each other from the beginning, and still to this day those two share a love that only they have between the two of them.

Luna wins the award among my dogs for the most escapes. She could run a ten-mile sled trip, come home, and somehow get out and still take off. I learned the hard way that an open window, no matter on what floor of my house, if it is open, she will jump out of it. Nor do screens stop her. I have replaced so many screens on my windows I could go into business. I did not have central air-conditioning in my house during those hot summer months, and the only way to cool down my house was to open the window. After we learned of her clever trick, we only opened the windows on the second floor.

She also would confirm that my dogs love to wait until I am in the shower to perform any of their escape attempts. They figure that I am occupied and not paying attention, which of course I'm not. I had just stepped out of the shower to see Luna standing in the hallway of my second floor. Directly across from the bathroom was my computer room, which had the window open. She looked at me, then the window, then me again, and just like that she bolted, jumped through my screen, landed, and took off. So there I went again, running after my dog while holding tightly to my bath towel and chasing her through my neighborhood. This little stunt of hers would happen one more time that week, and again it sent me chasing her in nothing but my bath towel.

We soon learned that one of the doors to one of my upstairs rooms would not lock when the door would shut. Luna would take any opportunity she could to get out. The instant the wind blew that bedroom door open, she was gone out the window. I was downstairs doing laundry when my doorbell rang. When I opened the door, there stood two neighborhood kids and Luna.

I was baffled by them. And then one of the kids asked, "Is she a stunt dog?"

I was confused, but then he told me he saw her jump out the second-story window and she must be a movie stunt dog. I laughed and said no, but she did have a talent for getting into a lot of trouble. Now that we are suffering in the sweltering heat of the summer and cannot open the windows, I was forced to purchase central air, which to everyone who has it, knows it's not cheap.

"I work to support my dogs" has become my new motto.

During this my time with the dogs, we relocated to a new house near a ski resort. I installed six-foot privacy fencing to deter the escape attempts of my little Luna. I fenced in the largest area my dogs have ever had, so they had lots of room to run around and play. My first winter at this house, we encountered record snowfall amounts. This snow came up halfway on the panels of the fence in the backyard. Luckily, it took Luna till February to learn that just one small jump away was freedom.

Naturally, of course, at this time I was recovering from a right elbow fracture that had required surgery. My mother stayed with me for two weeks to help me take care of the dogs as well as myself. One evening my mother stepped out to the front porch to get some snow for my ice pack, and well, wouldn't you know, there was Luna. She had jumped the fence, ventured around long enough to get bored, and then came back.

So, from there on out, it was my mother and I walking Luna around the front yard to get her to go to the bathroom. She, of course, would NEVER go! So we took her to the backyard. Luna would urinate on a leash but never option number two. We devised a hillbilly plan. I would walk her out to the front yard on a leash, my right arm in a full-arm cast and sling, with my mother armed at the other end where she had been jumping out. My poor mother had a leaf rake. When Luna came her way, she would wave it around and holler! It would scare the dickens out of Luna and she would come back to the other area of the backyard.

Each time we let Luna out she would always slightly look right, scanning to see if the leaf rake woman was still there. She would stop, stare, and let out a loud exhale. It was like she was saying, "Crap! They have me figured out!"

Three weeks after my surgery, I had to go home to Lansing with my parents. That way they could work and yet still help me with the dogs. Opening anything was unsuccessful, I couldn't carry all the dog food without spilling it, I was unable to open Panda's medication, etc. Let's face it; I wasn't able to do much. I knew Luna had escaped their fence many times before. So while there she would have to go out on her leash.

On the second day we were there, she got out. I had walked her out, slipped, and for fear of falling on my right arm, I dropped her leash. In two seconds she was to the fence and gone. I bolted inside, threw on my dad's slippers, and grabbed my car keys. Now, I had not been driving yet. It is kind of difficult to drive a full-sized truck, in the winter, without your dominant arm. Luna was running from house to house and ignoring me. I eventually chased her about a mile down the road to a fire department. It was there that I cornered her and caught her. But when I went back to my truck, it wouldn't start. I had run out of gas.

I had been in such a hurry to chase after her that I'd forgotten my cell phone. Now, remember I do not have a working arm, and it is in a full-sized cast. So doing my hair doesn't happen. Curly, untamed hair can be quite a sight. I had to wear my father's oversized sweatshirts because my arm cast would not fit in any of mine. I also was wearing oversized sweatpants because I was not able to button up my jeans. I imagine I looked like one hot mess. I encountered three people on my walk back to the house, and all three turned me down when I asked for a cell phone.

So Luna and I started our long, cold, hobbling walk home. I had no coat on, I was wearing my dad's oversized slippers, my right arm appeared to be missing under my oversized sweatshirt, and my hair was flying in ninety directions. I walked her all the way home, meeting my father en route. He saw my truck was gone and knew what had happened. He took me back to my truck and filled it with enough gas to make it to the gas station. I took Luna home, and when I opened the door to let the other dogs in, I was jumped on. I dropped her leash, and away she went again. That was the start to my two-hour downtown Lansing Luna chase. We did eventually catch her, and she was under careful watch after that.

When I returned home, I was going to be on my own with my broken arm. To help keep Luna in the yard, my mother and father added snow fencing to the top of my existing six-foot-high fence. They built it across the area where the snow had drifted so high it turned my fence into a two-foot-high fence. They spent over an hour in the blistering cold, the wind, and falling snow to install this fence. Once it was up, we let Luna out. She stood in the middle of my yard and stared down that section of fencing. Then, like a horse out of the gates, she went full speed toward the fence line. She was not able to clear the added height, but that didn't discourage her. She just decided to climb an entirely new section of fencing. I think my parents stood there, jaws dropped. Yup, she really just did that. So, back to Luna and me leash walking her with a broken arm for her bathroom breaks.

My little sister moved in with me, and with her came her many pairs of shoes. My dogs have always left my shoes alone, but it may be because I have always taken care of my shoes so they are not in the reach of their teeth. Lisa, being new to the pack, was used to leaving her shoes by the door when she came in. Luna would develop a taste not just for any of my sister's shoes, but for the expensive ones. I felt awful, but my theory is that after the first pair is destroyed, you should know the tactics so put your shoes away. Simple solution, if you ask me. Lisa did, and Luna then opened her closet door and still stole them. I did feel bad that my dog was creating these kinds of problems, and it seemed to only be my sister's shoes she would continually go after. She consumed at least five pairs of my little sister's shoes before Lisa child-proofed an area where her shoes were then kept. At least Luna had good taste, because only the expensive leather or suede shoes would appeal to her stomach.

Luna has been my most expensive dog, even though I got her for free. This is not due to what she has cost herself, but in the preventive measures she has forced me to take. One morning I arrived home from work to find that I had all six of my dogs staring at me from my picture window. I was very perplexed by this because I had locked them in the kennel in my backyard when I had gone to work the night before. I knew that Malakai was the culprit who let them in my house, but how did they all get out of the kennel? When I entered the back-yard, I saw that the kennel had been chewed through. The kennel was made up of chain-link fencing. A large hole had been made in the wire near the bottom of the kennel door.

I began to assess each dog to make sure that no one had received an injury while getting out. Everyone was fine, except something was wrong with Luna. She was limping and not being her usual excited self. I looked over her legs and could not find a source of any injury. It was when she rolled over to her back that I saw what was causing her pain. She had impaled herself in her chest area on the chain-link fence. I placed the rest of my dogs in the house and rushed her to the emergency vet. Luckily they were not busy that early in the morning. Luna was seen very quickly, and a plan was made that she would have to go back for surgery. Later that day I received a phone call that I could come and pick her up. When I arrived they informed me that she had torn through three layers of muscle that was all stitched back together, and a Penrose drain had to be placed to help remove the flu-ids. Luna then came home with me and recovered good as new.

Due to Luna's heroic escape, I was forced to build a kennel that was Luna-proof. My father built what I like to call the "Alcatraz" of all dog kennels. It has a deck floor on the outside portion of the kennel and a full wooden floor on the inside. The walls were made of six-foot wooden planks with steel hog-wire windows to allow air flow. Luna would not be able to climb, chew, or dig out of this one. Therefore Luna cost me the expenses of surgery and a new kennel, all in one month's time.

One morning while I was hooking the dogs up to head out for a run, we ran into a few problems right at the start. At this point, anchoring to the F-150 was working very well with the quick release. But when we took off, my two lead dogs became intertwined in the lines and I was going to need to stop. My neighbors just so happened to be getting into their car at that moment and bore witness to the events unfolding. I was not able to leave the brake because the excitement in the team at the start of the run is very intense and they would have taken off with the cart if I got off. I was giving commands that seemed to be ignored.

My neighbor meanwhile was telling my dogs, "Children, children, listen to your mother."

I was laughing at this because her presence was only making the dogs more excited, and they were being referred to as "my children." This carried on for what seemed like forever. She would speak to them in a stern manner, hands on her hips and finger pointing at them. I was still on the cart, attempting to calm them down, but with no luck. She then proceeded to come over to my driveway and offered to stand on the cart and hold the brake while I went to untangle my leads.

"Children, children, you listen to your mother!" she would say. "Children, she is trying to help you, you better behave."

All that flashed through my mind was me getting off the cart and my neighbor getting taken for the ride of her life. In the end my two leads untangled themselves on their own, and we were off like a bat out of hell.

Luna, along with Malakai, has also become a fan of eating my trees. It was the summer that I was making progress with the landscaping in my yard. I had just bought and planted a beautiful twelve-foot crabapple tree that was blossoming. The branches from the bottom started about five feet up the tree. One day I was walking through my house and just happened to look out my back door. What I saw still absolutely astounds me. There, hanging in midair, clutching one of the tree branches in her mouth, was Luna. She was swaying in the air, all four feet swinging below her and shaking my poor tree in an attempt to tear off the limb. I caught her in time, and she was not successful, but eventually the tree did fall victim to Luna and the limbs were removed.

Luna takes every opportunity she can to run loose through the town. As many husky owners have encountered, they love to stay just out of your reach, as if to say, "Nah-nah-nah-nah-boo-boo." Luna was playing this game for over an hour, following my car but staying just out of reach. She followed me repeatedly over the same few blocks of my neighborhood until I had a genius idea. My dogs are overly friendly and love to greet people. So I got the great idea and walked into my town bar. Luna stopped about fifteen feet away from the door with her head cocking from side to side, trying to figure out where I was going. I went in, opened the door, then stood in the doorway and called her. The giddy-up she had on her gait made me laugh. She was coming full-tilt into that bar. When she reached the door, I grabbed her. I know she thought, *Oh crap!! I've been outsmarted!* Then Luna and I proceeded to my car, but I could only think the people of the bar thought I was nuts.

Although Luna has proven to be the most costly dog I have ever owned, she is a loving, high-energy, spirited little pup. I am so excited that she has entered my life. Luna is great with other dogs, children, and other adults. She has been an amazing asset to my sled team, being my fastest and smartest in the lead positions. Luna has been a joy since she came into my house, and I am looking forward to the many memories we will make together.

Supermodel (Luna's Story)

Well, I must say that the start of my life was not the best. I was purchased as a puppy by a family that didn't understand my needs. I bounced around to a few more houses at my young age, and then ended up with the best person in the world. She understood me and what I needed. The first day I lived at her house, she took me out running. I ran with the rest of her canines and followed their lead, but I was in heaven. I could run forever.

Running is my life. Sometimes she can take me running for miles, and when we get back to the house, I want to go for more. I am a skilled climber and the fenced-in area we play in is no problem for me to climb over. I don't want to bother her so I don't mind letting myself out. There is nothing better than roaming through the neighborhood, saying hi to the fellas, and running to my heart's content. She attempts to follow me in her rumbling piece of metal, but I'm usually not ready to go with her when she finds me. I love to follow her through town, but I stay just out of reach. That way we can see the town together.

She leaves so many opportunities for me to stretch my legs. There are windows in her house that she likes to leave open when it's hot out in the summer. Well, there is only a thin piece of fabric keeping me inside. So I just run through the fabric. No biggie. That way she doesn't have to let me outside herself, and it saves me the hassle of having to wait for her to take me out running herself. She thought she would get creative and stop me by keeping the windows closed on the lowest floor of the house and only leave the windows open on the top floors of the house. If only she understood that I have never had a fear of heights. Being as high as I can be is actually my favorite. I like being above everything because it gives me a sense of empowerment.

She plants these trees all the time in her yard, and despite Malakai's constant destruction, she keeps planting them. Well, after Malakai removed four trees, she planted a taller one. That one was my favorite because it had branches that were close to ground, but just out of reach. I had to jump on them to grab them. I could hang on with my teeth and swing around. It was so much fun to be so high in the air. This made it seem like it was my own personal swing. Malakai was always on the ground yelling at me to get down. Why does she always think that she gets to be in charge?

Malakai always has thought that she was the top girl because she was the only one. Well, I have a slimmer waistline; I have the bright blue eyes and the shiny white coat. Everyone knows that blondes have more fun and are prettier. I'm sorry, Malakai, but I am better and faster than you. She has always tried to knock me off the pedestal that I have earned among this new pack, but fat chance of that, Malakai.

I am the master escape artist. Once I did it, like, fifty times, I decided I loved it, and I would try to get out of everything I was ever put into: like a car, a crate, a bedroom, a bathroom, a bathtub, a harness, a collar, or even my own personal-built dog hotel. I admit there wasn't much that I couldn't get out of. I even chewed my way through a chain-link fence! Yeah, I got hurt but the girl took care of me. The consequence of that action was that she had someone build a large area with wooden floors, wooden walls, and super strong chain for the windows. Touché, lady, I was stuck. She was kind enough to give us our own personal pool and fan in there, so that made it fun to go in. I swear one day I will find my way out.

I love my life with her and my family. There are so many opportunities to go out and run, and I always get to be in the front. I have

learned so many commands and can execute each one with no problem. She is proud of me, I know, because she tells me so a lot. I also
hear "naughty girl" a lot, too, but I figure she doesn't really mean
that. Everything is good at our home. I met lots of new dogs, and
new people, and I get lots of love. I know I push her limits sometimes, but she has the most forgiving heart of anyone I have ever met.

Katori

Katori has been the newest addition to my pack. She was about seven months of age when I got her. She was given to me by a family who understood that they could not care for a breed like the Siberian husky. Katori would take advantage when her small children would open the door and she would bolt out. That can be a very dangerous situation for any dog. Luckily, I was contacted, and I went and picked her up.

When I arrived, Katori was living in a trailer park. This was a risky situation with her, because there is a lot of traffic coming in and out the park. As many times as she had escaped, she was at risk of getting hit by a car. I brought Kodah and Malakai with me because they are my best at meeting new dogs. The houses were very close to each other with not much room for a yard of any kind. Katori was tied up outside to the only tree by the house. She was a shy little puppy, afraid of Kodah at first. She eventually warmed up to him, though, and I allowed Malakai to then meet her. Two dogs definitely overwhelmed her, and she became fearful. Kodah and Malakai could sense her uneasiness and backed away. In time she became more comfortable with them, and I placed her in my car and we headed for home.

Katori has sassiness in every aspect of her. She is a beautiful white Siberian husky with gentle brown eyes. Katori is now full of spirit and energy. This little girl can go ninety miles an hour twenty-four hours a day. She has proven to be that little bit of extra energy that my teams need when they start to get tired. Katori is now an expert hole digger, dog toy destroyer, and my new official dishwasher pre-rinse cycle. She is a loving girl who is ready to explore the world.

She has developed somewhat of an attitude problem since I got her. She takes Rhyno's talking back at me to a whole new level. Katori has developed selective hearing, meaning she does not always listen to me. Sometimes she will give me attitude before I have even caught on to what she has done.

Our first season of performing dogsled rides, a local news crew covered our story. The man had many cameras, large and small, to get as many angles as possible. He took cameras deep into the course and placed them along the trails. Some of the cameras that he placed were GoPros, which thankfully are shockproof and waterproof. Well, little Miss Katori thought he had placed random toys along the trail for her to pick up. We got an excellent view of dogsledding from inside Katori's mouth. They thought it was so funny, it actually aired in two different segments!

I am thankful that I have not had Katori for that long to have any stories to really tell about her. It does not mean that she won't have some things in store for me in the future. I can only hope that the other dogs have trained me well over the years as to what this breed is truly capable of, and preventive measures are in place. I look forward to the many years and experiences that I will get to share with her and the rest of my pack.

Squirrel! (Katori's Story)

Since the day I came into this world, I just have had to go, go, go, go. It's what I do and all I know. The lady rescued me when I was just a young girl and brought me to live with her family of canines. The very first day I came, she took me out running with the rest of them, and I had so much fun. But it was hard not to be distracted by everything. There was a tree here, a leaf there, and people. Oh my gosh! There were so many people. I would look this way and look that way, and sometimes I would get dizzy because I couldn't keep up with all the new sights and sounds. Luna was amazing—she could take all the new encounters in without ever flinching from the lady's commands. Someday, I want to be like Luna. After all, the two of us are both blondes.

I have the opportunity at my new house to go out and go running a lot. The lady ried to let me run up front with Luna, but I guess running off the trail every ten feet is frowned upon. I then got moved to the back, which stank, because she was right there behind me. It's hard to have any fun when she is that close. When we get harnessed up, I am just beside myself. I can't sit still, I can't stop my body from wiggling, I talk, talk, talk, talk, talk, and then she tells me to calm down, but I just can't, it's too hard.

People leave the most outrageous things lying around; it can be downright appalling. I love finding new things, and for every new thing that I find, I like to put in my mouth first to make sure it's not edible. I have to be first on my feet to get every scrap of food at whatever cost. When you live with as many canines as I do, you need to be quick or else it's gone in the blink of an eye.

There is only one problem that I have with my life situation. When we go running, I am the only one that gets through-the-roof excited. It's not my fault, I just can't contain it. The lady lets everyone else get harnessed and hooked up to the sled, and she makes me wait until last. It's pure torture to watch all of my canine family get hooked up first and I have to wait. Would she like to be the last one fed at dinnertime? No, I don't think so. So by the time I come out, it's too hard not to scream and jump in excitement. I just want to run and get going now. She pairs me next to Rhyno, and he just doesn't understand my thought processes sometimes. He is always telling me to calm down, slow down, take it easy, but I can't. Once my harness is hooked up, it's like my legs have springs. I can't stop them from bouncing off the ground over and over. Let's run, let's go, let's go now!! Once I am running, I am finally at peace. My mind can slow down…a little… and my heart is experiencing pure joy.

My life is a grand one filled with so many new things. The lady takes us places all the time, lets us go running, and feeds us so many yummy goodies. It's a sensory overload at times, and I have to dial things down a bit to take it all in, but life is truly fascinating. I am so excited to have come to her so young because I can only imagine what's to come.

Dartanian

Dartanian is the sweetest, gentlest of souls among my pack of pups. I adopted him from an animal shelter. Dart was found tied to a mailbox in the middle of nowhere. Thankfully someone found him and took him to the shelter so he could get that second chance at life. Dartanian has one blue eye and one brown eye and a deep red, coarse coat. He adapted the day I got him in my pack, and I am so thankful he joined my family.

Dartanian has speed, energy, and enthusiasm for running like no other dog on my team. When you see him standing in line waiting to go, he is patient, sitting still, but when the dogs take off, you get a powerhouse. Dart runs swing position (behind a lead dog) most of the time, but I have high hopes for training him to be a lead dog. Right now everything is so fun and new, he reminds me of the dog from the movie *Up*: "Squirrel!"

Dartanian was not a fan the day I put him in the kennels in my basement. My father built eight-foot-by-ten-foot kennels for them to stay in when I go to work. They have wood walls on all sides to keep in those that like to chew chain-link fence. Well, Dart thought half-inch wood was also a chewable substance. He managed in an eight-hour shift to chew an entire hole the diameter of his head out of my kennel door. My father had to redo the door to the kennel entirely, and I had to place a different dog in the kennel with him to occupy him. Turns out that was all he wanted, not to be alone.

I have not had Dartanian long at this point in time, but he has been a joy to have around. I have high hopes for this young dog. He acts like he does not have a care in the world, and I am so excited to see what this boy can do.

This Is Awesome (Dartanian's Story)

I found happiness the day that the lady came to get me from the animal shelter. I had been found tied up to a pole with a box on top of it. Some nice people came and found me, and they took me to the animal shelter, where I waited for months for her to come and get me. The animal shelter was a nice place, though. They had many people come and take me for a walk every day, I got a clean kennel every day, and I had food! Oh, I love food! I love food so much. It's the best thing next to my new home that I have ever experienced.

The lady who came to get me from the shelter brought two dogs with her named Malakai and Kodah. They were the nicest dogs that I have ever met. They showed me space and kindness because I was a little nervous meeting new dogs. The lady then put me in her rumbling, metal machine and took me home, only to meet more dogs. I got to meet them one at a time because there were a lot of them to meet. They were all so nice and told me many stories about how life was great there. The area she put us all in was huge! I could run full speed and make laps. I have never been able to run that free and fast before. The young girls in the group are just as fast as I am, and I love to chase them around all the time. I had finally come to the perfect place for me.

All the other dogs and I get the chance to go out and run! It is so awesome! We run so fast and for so long that I can finally sleep comfortably. I have never been able to put my mind to rest like that before. It made me realize how much I needed to exercise, because I was a happy camper when I did. The lady took us to meet lots of people, and they got to come running with us, too. There were little people who giggled and smiled at me all the time, too! I like them the most because they seem so happy all the time. Well, there was one little person who cried and screamed when the big person said it was time to go and let someone else have a turn. Oh man, the decibels that his screams could get to almost could break my ears. The big person carried him away, and he was still kicking and screaming. Only the little people did stuff like that; the big people never did.

I have been training alongside Luna up front for a while now. She has been great and patient, helping me learn the ropes of running as a lead dog. There are so many things that the lady says to us, but Luna knows them all. She is so smart, and I hope that I can be as good as she is someday. Luna understands how to set the pace for the team. She recognizes when they are getting tired and we need to slow down, or when a herd of deer are running across our path and we need to keep the team from running in the woods. Someday I will be that good, and I will make the lady proud, too.

My new home is absolutely heaven on earth for me. I get plenty of exercise, socialization, and treats. The lady loves to buy us treats. She only gives them to us when she says it's bedtime. But that's okay because then I get to sleep next to her on the soft plush bed. I was rescued the day that she came to the shelter to get me. That is the day my life began.

Cozumel

Cozumel is a frequent visitor to my team. She is a Rottweiler mix that my sister owns. Cozy has been running with us since she was a year old. Most people are amazed and baffled when they see her on a dogsled team, but she loves it. She is actually one of the craziest, excited dogs to run.

Most people think that only the Nordic breeds like the Alaskan malamute or Siberian husky, can pull a dogsled, but that is not true. If you monitor the temperatures, hot or cold, any dog that wants to pull -can do it. Cozumel actually is capable of running as a lead dog next to Luna. My sister has told me that when Cozumel sees the harness, she goes nuts. My sister, Lisa, has to harness her in her bedroom because she is known to jump on anything that is tall due to her excitement.

Cozumel learned how to dogsled from my dogs. She knows the commands, she loves the sport, and she brings a new speed to my team. You will find Cozumel running alongside my team often because she loves to run.

Urban Dogsledding

For all of you out there who do not get to experience winter but do have a chance at cooler weather, urban dogsledding is for you. There are carts and scooters made specifically for dogsledding in the months when there is no snow. They are usually built based on the number of dogs that you run, but you can usually find them in most states. The Internet is a great way to find local businesses that sell the equipment. Biking is also another great way to get dogs out sledding when there isn't any pretty white stuff to cover the ground. Any breed of dog can sled. I run often with my sister's Rottweiler mix, and one of my rescue dogs is more lab than husky, but they still love to run!

I use a three-wheeled cart for the spring, summer, and fall months. It is a cart designed for teams of four to six dogs. It has a push brake for the back two tires; it is a stand-on cart, with a handlebar for steering. The cart weighs about ninety pounds and is four feet tall and four feet wide. The front tire is mainly for steering while the back two tires provide traction for the brake to stop the cart. I go through a lot of tires with the amount of braking that I have to do. The brake rubs directly on the tires, so the tread wears out fast. The axles take their fair share of work, too. My axles are replaced at least once a season. Over the years of wear and tear, I have had to replace all parts of my equipment. One realizes what works better than other products and which ones hold up longer.

Summer carts are an excellent way to prepare the team for winter. Getting the dogs in shape in the fall helps the winter months run smoothly. In the front of my summer cart is an area made specifically for the gangline to attach to. The gangline is your main line that runs through the dogs. The line that attaches to each dog's collar is called a neckline. The neckline helps to keep the dogs in tight formation while out running. The tugline is the line that connects to the back of each dog's harness. This is the line that gives the dogs the ability to get the sled moving.

I also have a large bungee attached to my line to help absorb the shock from stopping and going. Each dog wears a specially fitted harness for him or her to help ensure that when they pull the cart, it does not put pressure in the wrong areas of their body. The most important part of my equipment is the quick release line. It is designed to anchor the team, and when I am ready to move, I release this line, allowing for a very smooth takeoff.

The carts are designed to go off paved roads and maneuver along trails throughout wooded areas. Some carts can only handle paved areas. An adequate brake system is necessary when you are working without snow. In the winter, you have a snow hook and a claw brake designed to slow or stop the dogs. They have excellent traction and assist in bringing the dogs to a stop. It is more difficult to stop the dogs in a cart. The brakes are wonderful, but at the start when my dogs are revved up, they can easily pull the cart with the brakes on.

We also go out on dusk trips, when the sun has started to settle, and we run the risk of not being seen by others. I always take them to where the traffic is nonexistent, such as trails in the woods. Each dog has a lighted LED collar that flashes bright blue. This allows others to see us coming and be aware to stop. I also wear a headlamp in case extra light is needed.

I had to train the dogs to run through town. It took a lot of patience and help. I had a friend ride their bike in front of us, and I followed with the dogs. The front dog was attached to the back of the bike. This helped to keep them running straight and in control, especially if a squirrel were to run out in front of us. Over the years the dogs have learned to run very well through town, and they obey commands when obstacles present themselves.

Another trick I developed late in my years of dogsledding is kayak sledding. I take my four water dogs and harness them, then attach them to my kayak. It allows us to still get exercise on those hot muggy mornings. I have life vests for the dogs so when we decide to swim to deeper water they are safe. This allows the dogs to walk along the shoreline and enjoy exercise while staying cool at the same time.

A Trip to the Veterinarian

Veterinary care is very important for all dogs no matter what breed they are. A yearly checkup with your veterinarian can help your dogs live a healthy and happy life. Your vet will be able to guide you with the care that your dog needs, with medications, and with tests that can be performed to assist in a healthy lifestyle.

Veterinary care is a must among all dog owners. There are many health concerns that one must attend to when owning a dog. Yearly vaccinations, samples, and preventive medications are a few of the important health requirements for all dogs. Ensuring they are receiving adequate caloric intake when exercising helps to keep them active. Diet is very important when maintaining the health of an active breed.

Veterinary care also includes grooming. Proper grooming for all Alaskan malamutes and Siberian huskies helps to keep their skin and coat healthy yearlong and reduces the amount of shedding in your house.

Now, taking seven dogs to the vet is a challenge, but taking seven Siberian huskies and Alaskan malamutes at once is a circus sideshow. I have a vet that I have used for many years, and I drive quite a distance to go and see him. He is the only one who is considerate of the financial cost of owning seven dogs. I make a yearly appointment and take them all down to see him. To make things easier, I shuttle three dogs at a time into his office. My first three usually are Rhyno, Kodah, and Luna. I first check the lobby for potential dogs or cats. When the coast is clear, we enter. I sign us in and we take a seat awaiting our turn.

In the lobby is a beautiful fifty-five-gallon fish tank filled with very large goldfish. They are swimming about their business, not paying much attention to onlookers. I am sure the fish have had many stares and fingers pointing on the glass and have learned to ignore them. However, Rhyno is a few sandwiches short of a picnic and is easily distracted by very minuscule things. His eye catches the fish swimming around. As he is the biggest of my dogs and the strongest, he drags me over to the tank with Mali and Kodah in tow.

First, he follows the fish around with his head, but his excitement only grows. Now he is jumping on his two hind feet, trying to figure out how he could possibly get these fish.

I have a million scenarios racing through my head. He will knock over the tank: well, my dogs would get wet and they could get hurt on the glass, but luckily we are at the vet. Or Rhyno would just kinda "fall in" the tank. Thank goodness we are called back to the examination room before he ever has a chance to put any of my fears in action.

When the first three have completed their checkup, I shuttle them out, pass by a group that had gathered in the waiting room, and listen to all their comments of "Wow, look at all those dogs! There are so many!"

I laugh to myself because they have no idea I am on my way to collect the other half. I put those three back in the car, I grab the last four. I shuttle them in, pass go, and head back to the exam room.

As I go by I hear their astonishment: "She has eight dogs!"

I chuckle to myself because that is the story of my life. Everywhere I go, I am the crazy dog lady.

Identification

I have all my dogs micro-chipped, and they wear identification tags. For anyone who owns a husky or who might want to own a husky, these two things are vital. For the amount of times they may get loose on you, you need to have a way for others to contact you once they have found them. Micro-chipping is a onetime very inexpensive way to permanently ID your dogs, and it assists others in locating their owners when found.

Foot Care

When running a team of sled dogs, it is very important to pay close attention to the care of their feet. The feet can get worn out and cause sores that require treatment. There are preventive ways to keep the feet safe and avoid any possible complications. Booties are made and designed specifically for the foot of a dog. They help to keep the feet padded and protect them from harmful chemicals that might linger in the snow. Prior to putting the booties on, you can coat your dog's feet in a protective barrier cream made specifically for sled dogs. It is available in many brands and sizes. Keeping sled dogs' feet in good condition is essential in helping them run the distance they want to go.

Heat Safety

onitoring the outdoor temperature is also very important for the Siberian huskies and Alaskan malamutes. They have such a strong desire to run that they will run their hearts out. Only going out when the temperature is at a certain degree will help prevent health complications from occurring while out sledding. I run my dogs in the summer months, as well. I have a special cart that we use and that is capable of traveling over dirt and paved terrain. I only run my dogs when the temperature is cool enough that I do not feel that heat stroke is a possibility. The morning hours, I have found, are the best times during late summer months to exercise the dogs. In the middle of the summer, I take them all swimming to keep them cool but also exercise them at the same time. I have taken a kayak out and harnessed the dogs up to it. They all have lifejackets that they wear, and they pull me around the shallows of the lakes. It is a sight for onlookers to see, but I tell you, the dogs absolutely love it.

There are many activities I can occupy my dogs with when the weather is not favorable for running. Siberians and malamutes love exercise, which is why it is so important to keep them safe when summer comes, but I always monitor them for heat exhaustion and possible heat stroke. I have strict limits on the temperatures I allow them to go out in and how long they are out in the heat.

Dating

Dating? Well, that is the most difficult topic to cover in my life. Owning a dogsled team has added to the reasons why I am still currently single. It's difficult when you meet someone and your first two questions are, "Are you allergic to dogs, and do you own a cat?" It definitely throws them at first, but at least I get my two most important questions answered. If they are allergic, it's never going to work. If they have a cat, they might as well drop it off at the humane society because it doesn't stand a chance living at my house with my dogs. The dating world and my sled team live two different lives.

There have been instances when I have invited someone over for dinner. I feel like I need the guy to sign a waiver or pay admission to enter my house. I am very considerate when they first arrive, and I attempt not to overwhelm the poor guy. I usually only have two dogs inside at the start, and I gradually add one dog and then another until the poor guy is completely coated in hair. I don't keep all the dogs inside when I have company over. I let the gentleman meet them all as kind of a test. I'm not that cruel to let the poor guy endure all of the dogs the entire night; I do kennel them or leave them in the backyard.

My dogs seem to be a good judge of character, too. It depends on the dog, but they usually let me know when they do not approve of someone. One gentleman who hung out for a little while longer than the others. However from the start Rhyno did not approve of him. He also had no problem with letting me know that.

I remember one evening I was cooking in the kitchen, and the poor guy was sleeping on the couch. We had both worked the night shift, so sleeping at odd hours was not unusual. I heard a low, deep growl coming from my living room and, thinking it was Malakai getting ready to have one of her tiffs, I ran in there. It was then that I discovered it was Rhyno. While the gentleman was sleeping soundly, Rhyno had placed his head on the couch, eye level with him, his lip curled, and he was growling…deeply. He must have thought he'd take a bite out of the guy while he was sound asleep. So there I was quietly yelling, "Rhinocerous, Rhinocerous, Rhinocerous." He took one look at me and slowly turned his gaze back a final time for one last lip curl, then reluctantly walked away. But he always looked back at the couch as if to say, "I will get my chance."

I remember thinking that could have totally turned out bad. Rhyno had never shown that kind of behavior before. It didn't take me long after that to realize that Rhyno's instincts were accurate. It didn't work out with that guy. Rhyno just trusted his instincts a lot sooner than I trusted mine.

Another gentleman who braved coming over to my house also got a greeting by my pack of dogs. I had Malakai in the house at first with Panda. Mali can be leery when first meeting people, but usually she warms up pretty quickly. When he entered she sniffed him from a distance but remained far away. Panda, however, took it upon himself to get up close and personal. Mal still kept her distance, surveying the guy from every angle. Then suddenly her hackles went up, and she started growling and barking. The guy tried to lower herself to her level and let her come to him, but it was no use.

I switched out Panda for Kodah, which usually seemed to work for Malakai when she was uncomfortable. Kodah is over-the-top annoying on most occasions when new people come to the house. He needs to be loud to draw attention to himself so they will come and pet him. That is if their eardrums have not burst! Still, even with him showing her this guy was harmless, she did not trust him. So, for the rest of the evening, Malakai kept herself between the kitchen island and the guy. She was careful to always have a barrier between them.

Needless to say, that one did not work out, as well, and it was back to just the dogs and me again.

-I remember another gentleman who tried to brave entering my house. He was from out of town and came to visit me in Traverse City. When he came to the house, all the dogs greeted him appropriately, and there was not a single one who showed any hint of disapproval. The day went by, and we went out and about on the town. When we returned home, however, I noticed a problem. The guy had left all his clothes in the guest bedroom. When I walked through the door, most of the clothes had been removed from his bag and were scattered throughout the house. Luckily, it was evident that none of them had been torn but I was still mortified. He asked if this was a common occurrence among my dogs and whether they did this often.

Nope, that had definitely never happened before.

Through the rest of the day, the guy seemed leery of the dogs, always keeping his eye on where they were. He asked many questions throughout the day regarding the dogs and why I chose to have so many. This poor guy never stood a chance after my dogs ransacked his bag. That night while he was sleeping, he accidently left the bedroom door open. My dogs took it upon themselves to investigate him even further. It was wintertime, and there were many blankets on the bed. I am sure they circled the bed, attempting to figure out what this guy was doing in their house. It wasn't long before they had grabbed hold of his covers and ripped them off the bed. He, of course, woke up, and the dogs came running back into my room. I found it comical, but he did not. I can understand the situation from his perspective: yes, it would be intimidating to be picked on by a pack of huskies. Needless to say, he cut his trip short and ventured home the next day.

I am aware that my dogs are always going to be a huge barrier in my life. But they are very much a part of my life. I enjoy every minute I spend with them, and I would never change that. Someday someone may fall in love with dogsledding and my pups as much as I have, but until then, I am as happy as a clam living with my sled pups. I can also kiss my chance of a vacation good-bye. Who is possibly going to be able to watch this group of dogs while I go away for a few days? Most hotels only allow two dogs per room, with an occupant in each room. Any chance of ever going on a vacation with anyone else also has been put to the side. I can see myself on a beach somewhere and the hotel waiter brings me a phone; it's my housesitter, saying, "They are all out and running the neighborhood!" Then it's the first flight out for me and back home to wrangle the dogs. I figure it would take about five people staying at my house twenty-four hours a day to keep my pack in balance without me there.

Some people have even asked me whether I even do want to get married. The answer is: "Yes, I do, but it has to be right." I love what I do with the dogs, and no matter how challenging it is to keep them, I would never trade it for anyone. I trust my dogs' instincts around people, and so far they have always been right. My past few dating experiences ended, and each time it was for the best.

My dogs attempt to play the father figure with me. (I know it may be a little more canine dominance than father-like.) It sometimes feels like I am a teenage girl again, seeking the approval of my family to date someone. The dogs are not too accepting of a man entering my life. It may be that they have just not approved of the ones that I bring home or they just do not approve of a man at all in my life. It has been the dogs and me for so long that they do not accept change easily. Nonetheless, it will all work out someday how it is supposed to work out, but for now, I am having fun and enjoying my life with the dogs.

Adoption

am a huge advocate for spaying and neutering pets, yet I am not one who is against breeding by any means. There are some breeds of dog that you will just not find in a shelter. A shelter dog and a pure-bred, pick-of-the-litter pup are actually no different. But since the puppies are going to find a home, why not adopt an adult dog who has passed the cute stage and whose owners did not care for them anymore?

If you have ever rescued a shelter dog, you will understand me when I say that they have a certain appreciation toward you throughout their lives. It's as if they know that you gave them a second, and sometimes a third chance in life. A rescued dog is forever grateful.

I am a huge fan of adoption. Siberian huskies and Alaskan malamutes need homes all over the United States. I rescued five out of my current six dogs, and I know that I will always rescue dogs in the future. There are so many families and individuals who get these dogs because they are so beautiful. My family was one of them. But research these breeds before you decide to get a dog. The more you know about them, the better off both you and the dog will be.

I have come to own most of my dogs by some form of rescue, and there are so many more out there that I wish I could save. However, I advise all potential owners to research this breed of animal before acquiring one. They require an active lifestyle, proper grooming, and monitored living arrangements. Siberian huskies can be a remarkable breed to own if you understand their needs.

Siberians and malamutes will always be in shelters due to their owners acquiring them and not realizing the requirements these breeds have. Most people who bring these breeds home do not look into the maintenance that is involved with their care. That is why so many of these beautiful dogs end up in the shelter. I have found two of my dogs at shelters: Malakai and Dartanian. Five of them were given to me by word of mouth: Kodah, Rhyno, Bandit, Katori, and Luna. And finally I basically would not let my brother give Panda back to me. Panda and Toby were with me for many years while my brother was away at college. I was selfish, and yes, I kept Panda, but luckily my brother was able to get the kind of dog he had always wanted.

I myself had been turned down by an adoption agency when I attempted to adopt a Siberian husky. I had letters of recommendation from my boss—at a doggy daycare!—and a letter from my vet stating I was a qualified owner. However, this adoption agency did not care for my preference in career choice as a nurse, the fact that I was single, and the fact that I dogsled. So I do understand that it can be difficult in some circumstances to adopt. This agency did not like that I worked twelve-hour shifts and the fact that I could marry and my husband might not like the dogs. They also thought that dogsledding was cruel. Well, if only they knew the quality of life I provided for my dogs, maybe they would have changed their minds.

The shelter was right; most dogsled teams that participate for sport kenneled their dogs outside and to a short chain attached to a doghouse or barrel used for shelter. The dogs have access to water and food, but they don't have much room to move about. Now keep in mind, these dogs are exercised daily and for long distances. They take a lot of time to recuperate when they are done. So a small living area for these dogs does not usually bother them. They are also used to this way of life; they do not know any different way to live.

Once the agency was informed that my dogs live a comfortable life for sled dogs, they allowed me to adopt Malakai. I laugh to myself, thinking that I am now the one with no room to move around! Of course I sent them many pictures of the activities Malakai began to experience when she came to live with me, such as her first trip to a dog bakery, swimming in Lake Michigan, her Halloween costume, and her first picture with Santa. I did not tell the agency that she had tried to eat Santa, however. I thought these pictures would put their minds at ease about where Malakai had gone, and they were thrilled to hear from me.

Life can change in an instant, and sometimes you may not be prepared. That is what makes it life. If it was all laid out in black and white, where would be the fun in that? I am a huge believer that everything happens for a reason, and I couldn't have ended up with a better group of dogs.

There are many more events and stories that have occurred in my life related to my dogs. I love each moment I have with them, and I am excited but nervous for more memories to come. My greatest joy in life is spending time with my dogs. Anyone who owns a dog can understand the true love that can be shared between an owner and a dog. It is not comparable to anything else. Dogs can be so loyal, and you build a never-ending relationship with them. I would not be who I am today without my dogs. I love who I am when I am with them.

Each day I have with my dogs, there is usually some event that occurs for me to write down in my notes. I love each of my dogs for their own unique personalities. Each dog brings their own sense of creativity to my life. They make my life fulfilled and full of love. My dogs have seen me through so many good and bad times. They have seen me when I wake up (which is not always pretty), and they have seen me at my best, but the thing I love the most is that no matter what, their loyalty never fails. I love each day that I have with them, and I would not trade our life for anything else.

CPSIA information can be obtained at www.ICGtesting.com
Printed in the USA
LVOW07s1804211114

414960LV00002B/312/P